GREAT QUOTATIONS
ON
RELIGIOUS FREEDOM

GREAT QUOTATIONS
ON
RELIGIOUS FREEDOM

Compiled and Edited by

ALBERT J. MENENDEZ and EDD DOERR

Prometheus Books

59 John Glenn Drive
Amherst, New York 14228-2197

Published 2002 by Prometheus Books

Inquiries should be addressed to
Prometheus Books
59 John Glenn Drive
Amherst, New York 14228–2197
VOICE: 716–691–0133, ext. 207
FAX: 716–564–2711
WWW.PROMETHEUSBOOKS.COM

06 05 04 03 02   5 4 3 2 1

Library of Congress Cataloging-in-Publication Data forthcoming

ISBN 978-1-57392-941-7

For SHIRLEY *and* HERENIA

CONTENTS

CONTENTS

ACKNOWLEDGMENTS

We appreciate the permission to quote lengthy parts of published material by James Luther Adams, Leo Pfeffer, and R. Freeman Butts. We are also grateful for suggestions from Florence Flast, Art Must, and other friends of religious liberty too numerous to list. We are also grateful to Teri Grimwood for her invaluable assistance in the preparation of this book and others we have published.

ABOUT
THE
EDITORS

Albert J. Menendez and Edd Doerr are among the leading experts on religious freedom and church-state relations issues. Between the two, they have published forty-eight books and well over two thousand articles, book reviews, and other items in scores of publications. Mr. Menendez's book *Religion at the Polls* was named one of the ten best books on religion for 1977 by *Newsweek* and he received the 1978 Religious Heritage of America award for outstanding community leadership. Mr. Doerr received the Eric M. Steel Memorial Award, the American Humanist Association's Humanist Pioneer Award for his work in defending separation of church and state, and in 2000 the Religious Coalition for Reproductive Choice's Courage, Commitment and Choice Judy Halperin Mensch Award. Mr. Menendez and Mr. Doerr together have spent more than sixty-five years as writers and editors.

INTRODUCTION

Religious liberty. Separation of church and state. Freedom of conscience. These long-sought ideals of enlightened civilizations are the focus for this collection of quotations designed for all who have an interest in this subject area— whether as a specialist or a casual peruser. The editors hope that teachers, scholars, clergy, legislators, writers, and others who from time to time address these vital issues will find a great deal of useful material for public discussions, speeches, or sermons.

A wide array of sources, covering many centuries of human thought, have been utilized to make this a truly comprehensive *vade mecum* of great thoughts and noble ideas that have stirred the souls and moved the consciences of generations past and present.

All manner of men and women have been included, from early church fathers to Enlightenment philosophers and American presidents, from popes to anticlerical European statesmen. Opinions on these subjects are as diverse as the individuals themselves.

Quotation books have, it seems to us, given insufficient attention to the contributions of women. While men have tended to dominate the worlds of religion and politics, where most church-state interaction has occurred, there have been a number of important statements by women. We have therefore made an effort to include as many women as possible in this collection.

The quotations gathered here are unique, a collection of materials not found in any other single source. They also are to an extent a product of over forty years of reading and professional investigation by the editors.

The sources of the material include: presidential letters and inaugural addresses, papal encyclicals, books, speeches, essays, church and rabbinical resolutions, pastoral letters of bishops, testimony before Congress, newspaper editorials, magazine articles, declarations of church councils, and court rulings.

The vast majority of these "great quotations" extol the virtues of religious liberty and church-state separation, but a few selections sharply disagreeing with these concepts have been included, primarily to show the depth of feeling and the virulence of expression employed by such individuals as Pat Robertson, W. A. Criswell, Jerry Falwell, and certain pre-Vatican Council II popes.

Since the United States has been the prime laboratory of experimentation and growth in this field, a certain American flavor will be discerned in the selection of materials. It is significant, we think, that twenty-seven of our presidents have made statements on this subject. (With the exception of Ronald Reagan's groundless comment about God's "expulsion" from public schools, the presidential utterances have been universally laudatory.)

A number of the quotes deal with the perennial problem of religion and politics in the United States, the relevance of which is self-evident each election season. Parochiaid, school prayer, abortion rights, and the appointment of a U.S. ambassador to the Holy See have all brought forth a flowering of instructive commentary.

A special feature of this book is a compilation of major judicial quotes that bear on religious liberty, from the *Davis v. Beason* ruling of 1872 to the present. Most of these are from the U.S. Supreme Court, but a number of federal appellate decisions and state supreme court rulings have also been included. The magnificent rhetoric of such towering Supreme Court Justices as William J. Brennan and William O. Douglas make stirring reading and will fill the reader with justifiable pride in the rightness and continuity of these opinions.

We hope that all who use this volume for reference and information will find it profitable and that it will reinforce and deepen their appreciation for these noble principles.

Finally, the breadth and depth of this collection of great quotations should dispel the notion, frequently articulated by spokespersons for sectarian special interests, that the principle of separation of church and state is a recent invention or one concocted or espoused mainly by "communists" or "religion-haters." Rather, it has been championed by an enormously wide spectrum of men and women of diverse religious, social, and political views.

To make this book "user-friendly," the quotations have been grouped in thirty subject areas, in which the quotations are arranged alphabetically. They are numbered for easy access. Several appendices are devoted to special subjects. The judicial quotations are arranged chronologically. An alphabetical index is provided for reader convenience.

Albert J. Menendez
Edd Doerr
February 2002

GREAT QUOTATIONS

ON
RELIGIOUS FREEDOM

ABORTION RIGHTS

1. Catholics for a Free Choice

We affirm the religious liberty of Catholic women and men and those of other religions to make decisions regarding their own fertility free from church or governmental intervention in accordance with their own individual conscience.

1975

2. Central Conference of American Rabbis

We believe that in any decision whether or not to terminate pregnancy, the individual family or woman must weigh the tradition as they struggle to formulate their own religious and moral criteria to reach their own personal decision. . . . We believe that the proper locus for formulating these religious and moral criteria and for making this decision must be the individual family or woman and not the state or other external agency.

As we would not impose the historic position of Jewish teaching upon individuals nor legislate it as normative for society at large, so we would not wish the position of any other group imposed upon the Jewish community or the general population.

We affirm the legal right of a family or a woman to determine on the basis of their or her own religious and moral values whether or not to terminate a particular pregnancy. We reject all constitutional amendments which would abridge or circumscribe this right.

1962

3. Rev. Robert F. Drinan

It is seldom appropriate for one group within a society to seek to insert their moral beliefs, however profoundly held, into a document designed for people of fundamentally differing views.

Boston Herald-Traveler, March 26, 1974
Then-Congressman Drinan was speaking in opposition to a
proposed constitutional amendment to outlaw abortion.

4. Patrick Johnston, California Assemblyman

The didactic function of the Catholic Church is worthy of consideration and respect. But, in a pluralistic society, it cannot dictate the judgments that others of good conscience make with respect to these issues [abortion].

San Francisco Examiner, July 1989

5. Sen. Edward M. Kennedy (D-Mass.)

I believe that religious witness should not mobilize public authority to impose a view where a decision is inherently private in nature or where people are deeply divided about whether it is. . . .

Americans are plainly and persistently divided about abortion . . . and the fiat of government cannot settle the issue as a matter of conscience or of conduct.

Address, National Religious Broadcasters. February 4, 1985

6. Lucy Killea, California Legislator

I believe in separation of church and state. I cannot as a public official impose my religious views on people who do not share those views.

Address, San Diego. November 1989

7. Lawrence Lader

Pluralism has always been basic to the social stability of the nation. It involves acceptance by all society of the importance of its parts. For Catholics, the election of John F. Kennedy to the presidency ensured their place in the pluralist tradition, proving that the Protestant majority no longer monopolized that political process. Yet, the Catholic hierarchy still rejects pluralism when many of its moral beliefs and dogmas are in dispute.

Politics, Power and the Church (New York: Macmillan, 1987), p. 9

8. Martha L. Minow and Aviam Soifer

Given the dramatically contrasting religious views about whether and when abortion is permitted or required, state statutes drastically curtailing access to abortion unacceptably interfere with constitutionally protected religious and private conscience. Missouri's ban against abortion in public facilities, its ban against counseling about abortions by public employees, and its pronouncements that life begins at conception impermissibly invade religious liberty and freedom of conscience. Even though the Missouri law makes no mention of religion, it violates the Free Exercise Clause of the First Amendment. Especially in this sensitive area of great religious concern, public orthodoxy must be restrained and private conscience must be protected. . . .

If this Court were now to overturn its consistent position and to invite state legislation constraining or prohibiting abortion, the result would be extensive and disturbing government embroilment with matters of private religious conscience. Religiously inspired proponents on all sides of this issue would besiege state legislators. State lawmakers would be consumed by the enormous divisions between and even within religious groups on the issue of abortion. Public spaces would be occupied by religious controversies likely to erupt in acts of intolerance and violence. It is just these dangers that the Free Exercise Clause meant to avoid. . . .

The Court's role in preserving the space for the free exercise of personal and religious conscience is never more crucial than where there is massive public turmoil surrounding the subject. Otherwise, majorities, and even effectively mobilized minorities, can invoke the power of the state to curb the religious freedoms of those they do not like. The *amici* joining in this brief attest to the profound, prayerful commitments of extraordinarily diverse religious groups to this vision of tolerance enacted in our Constitution. . . .

It is not by accident that this Court's historic protections for families draw on both notions of individual privacy and notions of religious liberty. Deciding whether to marry or divorce, and whether to conceive and bear a child are simultaneously matters of individual choice and religious significance. The Constitution has provided, and must continue to assure, protection against governmental arrogation of crucial decisions which require the guidance of religious teachings and individual conscience.

Excerpts from *amicus curiae* brief to the U.S. Supreme Court
in *Webster* v. *Reproductive Health Services*, representing 36
Protestant, Catholic, Jewish, and other religious organizations, 1989.

9. Religious Coalition for Abortion Rights

The Religious Coalition for Abortion Rights is composed of thirty national religious organizations—Protestant, Jewish, and other faith groups. We hold in high respect the value of potential life; we do not take the question of choice lightly.

Because each denomination and faith group represented among us approaches the issue of choice from the unique perspective of its own theology, members hold widely varying viewpoints as to when abortion is morally justified. It is exactly this plurality of beliefs which leads us to the conviction that the abortion decision must remain with the individual, to be made on the basis of conscience and personal religious principles, and free from governmental interference.

Therefore we reaffirm the Supreme Court ruling of 1973, *Roe* v. *Wade*, which permits a woman to make a decision regarding abortion based on her own conscience and religious beliefs. We oppose efforts to enact into secular law one particular religious doctrine on abortion or the beginning of human life.

Statement to the U.S. Supreme Court in *amicus curiae* brief in
Webster v. *Reproductive Health Services*, 1989.

10. Governor Nelson A. Rockefeller

I do not believe it right for one group to impose its vision of morality on an entire society.

Veto message, May 13, 1972.
Rockefeller vetoed a bill to repeal New York's 1970 abortion law.

11. Rev. William F. Schulz, President, Unitarian Universalist Association

The question as to when full human life begins is a theological question upon which different religions differ. To allow state legislatures to adopt one definition over another and to force all of us to conform to one theological standard is nothing short of religious totalitarianism.

Remarks issued after the *Webster* decision
of the U.S. Supreme Court, July 1989.

12. Union of American Hebrew Congregations

The UAHC reaffirms its strong support for the right of a woman to obtain a legal abortion on the constitutional grounds enunciated by the Supreme Court in its 1973 decision. . . .This rule is a sound and enlightened position on this sensitive and difficult issue, and we express our confidence in the ability of the woman to exercise her ethical and religious judgment in making her decision.

The Supreme Court held that the question of when life begins is a matter of religious belief and not medical or legal fact. While recognizing the right of religious groups whose beliefs differ from ours to follow the dictates of their faith in this matter, we vigorously oppose the attempts to legislate the particular beliefs of those groups into the law which governs us all. This is a clear violation of the First Amendment. Furthermore, it may undermine the development of interfaith activities. Mutual respect and tolerance must remain the foundation of interreligious relations.

Biennial Convention, 1975

13. Right Rev. O'Kelly Whitaker et al.

As bishops of the Episcopal Church we have several concerns about the Missouri statute. We know that scientists, ethicists, theologians, and other faithful persons differ about the time that life begins, and we worry when states attempt to answer existential questions by statute. Similarly, we recognize the decision to have or not to have an abortion is a profound and personal decision to be made by the moral agent involved (that is to say, by the pregnant woman). We must object to any statute which would deny an individual the information necessary to make an informed decision about her reproductive health or the ability to act upon that decision.

From statement to the U.S. Supreme Court in *amicus curiae* brief in
Webster v. *Reproductive Health Services*, by six Episcopal bishops, 1989.

BLUE LAWS

14. Thomas Paine

The word Sabbath means rest; that is, cessation from labor, but the stupid Blue Laws of Connecticut make a labor of rest, for they oblige a person to sit still from sunrise to sunset on a Sabbath-day, which is hard work. Fanaticism made those laws, and hypocrisy pretends to reverence them, for where such laws prevail hypocrisy will prevail also.

The Prospect (1804)

CHAPLAINS

15. President James Madison

Besides the danger of a direct mixture of religion and civil government, there is an evil which ought to be guarded against in the indefinite accumulation of property from the capacity of holding it in perpetuity by ecclesiastical corporations.

The establishment of the chaplainship in Congress is a palpable violation of equal rights as well as of Constitutional principles.

The danger of silent accumulations and encroachments by ecclesiastical bodies has not sufficiently engaged attention in the U.S.

From the "Detached Memoranda." See Elizabeth Fleet,
"Madison's Detached Memoranda," *William and Mary Quarterly* 3 (1946): 554–62.

16. ———

Is the appointment of Chaplains to the two Houses of Congress consistent with the Constitution, and with the pure principle of religious freedom? In strictness the answer on both points must be in the negative. The Constitution of the

United States forbids everything like an establishment of a national religion. The law appointing Chaplains establishes a religious worship for the national representatives, to be performed by Ministers of religion, elected by a majority of them, and these are to be paid out of the national taxes. Does this not involve the principle of a national establishment . . . ?

"Essay on Monopolies" unpublished until 1946,
cited in Irving Brant, *The Bill of Rights*, (Indianapolis: Bobbs-Merrill, 1965).

CHARITABLE CHOICE

17. Rev. Scott Alexander, Senior Minister, River Road Unitarian Church, Bethesda, Md.

My congregation is passionately committed to social justice and human service work in the Washington community. We have fifteen active task forces that donate thousands of volunteer hours and more than $150,000 annually to providing affordable housing and food to the poor, funding minority college scholarships, and offering after-school ministry to D.C. youth.

Nonetheless, most of my congregation and I are extremely wary of President Bush's faith-based initiative. As one of the country's minority religions, we are gravely concerned about which religious and faith-based programs would be "approved" for funding, and which would not be. By what theological, moral or programmatic standards are federal officials going to decide whether the prison ministry they fund will be run by evangelical Christians, Black Muslims, the Church of Scientology, Buddhists, Presbyterians, Mormons or Unitarian Universalists? Perhaps the president does not fully grasp how diverse religious beliefs are in these United States, and maybe he's forgotten that more than 50 percent of Americans have no formal religious affiliation at all.

Compassionate congregations like the one I'm so proud to serve will continue to do their part, alongside secular human services agencies, to address the social ills of our nation. But let's not expand the role federal dollars play in faith-based programs, which need to do their work as free as possible of interference, prejudice or conflict.

Washington Post, February 18, 2001

18. James M. Dunn, Executive Director, Baptist Joint Committee, 1981–1999

When government claims to aid all religions, it never fails to play favorites.

Report from the Capital (October 1985)

19. Rep. Chet Edwards (D-Tex.)

America's gift of religious freedom is one of the most wonderful gifts our democracy has given to the world, and we should tinker with that principle with great trepidation.

Report from the Capital (February 7, 2001)

20. Marci A. Hamilton

When religions step into the shoes of the government, the civil rights of those receiving the funds become an issue. In order for the transmission of funds to be constitutional, the government will be required to place limits on how the funds are administered, including limitations on proselytization. Such limits, though, invite free-exercise challenges from the churches. Government funding in any category implicating First Amendment values invites discord and litigation.

"Religion and the Law in American Politics," in Mark Silk, ed., *Religion and American Politics: The 2000 Election in Context* (Hartford, Conn.: Center for the Study of Religion in Public Life, 2000), p. 84.

21. Rev. Wanda Henry, Baptist Joint Committee Administrator

Say "no thank you" to government funds for your religious ministries. You are doing just fine without the heavy hand of government on your back. . . .Charitable Choice threatens to make religion the servant of the state.

Report from the Capital (February 7, 2001)

22. Elena Matsui and Joseph Chuman

[Charitable choice] will turn religion against religion. It will make religion a servant of the state. It will let our government play favorites among believers, and it will destroy the separation of church and state as we have known it. . . .

[A]ny true friend of religion would be very wary of Charitable Choice for the threats it augurs for religious freedom. Scores of national religious organizations and hundreds of religious leaders across the religious spectrum, from conservative to liberal, have signed on against Charitable Choice. . . .

Proselytization will become rampant—at taxpayer expense. . . .

The judiciary will be forced to pass theological judgment and draw distinctions between one religion and another to determine which is government certifiable and which is not. . . .

Charitable Choice will have houses of worship competing against each other for bountiful government contracts. . . .

If government regulation is lax, it will invite the use of funds for narrowly sectarian purposes. . . . If oversight is rigorous, churches will routinely have to explain and defend their fiscal policies to government agents. . . . It was this type of subordination of religion to the state that the framers of the Constitution feared most when they crafted the religious freedom clause of the First Amendment. . . .

Under Charitable Choice, employees of churches that hire them will have no security, no federal protection or redress. . . .

We believe that religion plays its most important social role when it stands outside the precincts of secular power and critiques the abuses of government from the plateau of higher moral ideals. Charitable Choice will function to domesticate religion and render it harmless.

Bergen Record, New Jersey, February 10, 2000. Elena Matsui was a student at Teaneck High School in New Jersey when this was written. Joseph Chuman is leader of the Ethical Culture Society of Bergen County.

23. Melissa Rogers

Our country is the most religiously vibrant in the world. This is no accident. Unlike so many other nations, religion in America relies on voluntary gifts, rather than compulsory tax funds. Unlike religion abroad, religion in this country is largely free from government direction and regulation. Charitable choice would undercut these foundations, causing religious freedom to suffer. We must fight hopelessness and poverty. We can and should do so without sacrificing religious liberty.

"The Wrong Way to Do Right: A Challenge to Charitable Choice," in *What's God Got to Do with the American Experiment?*, ed. E. J. Dionne Jr. and John J. Diiulio Jr. (Washington, D.C.: Brookings Institution Press, 2000), p. 145.

24. ———

Charitable choice attempts to obliterate any legal distinction between religiously affiliated and pervasively religious organizations, allowing both to receive tax funds.

Ibid., p. 139

25. Paul D. Simmons

Those who advocate public support for clergy or religious enterprises have not come to terms with the corrupting and enervating effect of governmental protectionism. . . . Efforts to protect lead to the corruption and weakening of religion by the civil powers.

Freedom of Conscience (Amherst, N.Y.: Prometheus Books, 2000), p. 57

CHRISTIAN NATION

26. President John Adams

As the government of the United States is not, in any sense, founded on the Christian religion; as it has in itself no character of enmity against the laws, religion or tranquility of Musselmen [Muslims] . . . it is declared . . . that no pretext arising from religious opinion shall ever produce an interruption of the harmony existing between the two countries.

Treaty with Tripoli, 1797. (The original language is by Joel Barlow, U.S. Consul, in *The Works of John Adams* [Boston: Little, Brown & Co., 1856], volume IX, p. 636.)

CHRISTMAS SYMBOLS ON PUBLIC PROPERTY

27. Rev. Robert F. Drinan

It is surely the quintessence of the spirit of Christmas that those who believe in the divinity of the infant in the crèche should not seek to impose their view on others who do not share that faith.

America (December 13, 1986): 375–76

28. Lois Waldman

Most Jews intuitively know that if the evangelical right succeeds in Christianizing America, Jews will again find themselves an isolated minority alien to American culture.

"After Pawtucket," American Jewish Congress (July 1985)

29. *Washington Post*

The answer lies in the common understanding we have as Americans about our diverse religious views and our respect for each other's beliefs. This tolerance binds us as a people and protects us as individuals. We have agreed that each person may practice his own religion without interference from the state, and we don't want the government to do anything that will promote one religion over another.

Let crèches appear on every church lawn in Rhode Island. Let the Pawtucket merchants' association build one out of marble. But keep the city council and the taxpayers' money on the other side of Thomas Jefferson's wall lest an intrusive government, eager to support the large majority, crowd out, separate and impose on others whose rights are sacred too.

Editorial (March 7, 1984)

CIVIL LIBERTY

30. President John Quincy Adams

Civil liberty can be established on no foundation of human reason which will not at the same time demonstrate the right to religious freedom. . . . The tendency of the spirit of the age is strong toward religious liberty.

Letter to Richard Anderson, May 27, 1823

31. Roland Bainton

Civil liberties scarcely thrive where religious liberties are disregarded and the reverse is equally true. Beneath them all is a philosophy of liberty which assumes a measure of variety in human behavior, honors integrity, respects the dignity of man, and seeks to exemplify the compassion of God.

The Travail of Religious Liberty (New York: Harper & Brothers, 1951), p. 175

32. Norman Dorsen

Zealous [religious] groups threaten to infringe civil liberties when they seek government support to impose their own religious views on nonadherents. This has taken many forms, including attempts to introduce organized prayer in public schools, to outlaw birth control and abortion, and to use public tax revenues to finance religious schools.

"Civil Liberties," from *Encyclopedia of the American Constitution*, edited by Leonard W. Levy, Kenneth L. Karst, and Dennis J. Mahoney (New York: Macmillan, 1986), p. 378.

33. Rev. Charles Turner

Religious liberty is so blended with civil liberty that if one falls it is not expected that the other will continue.

Duxbury, Mass., Election Sermon, 1773

34. John Witherspoon, President of Princeton University, Signer of the Declaration of Independence

God grant that in America true religion and civil liberty may be inseparable.

Address at Princeton, May 17, 1776

CIVIL RELIGION

35. Robert S. Alley

The present emphasis upon civil religion is a flagrant toying with the First Amendment. Various trends in national life suggest that a civil religion of the majority might find religious liberty something it did not care to preserve.

So Help Me God (Richmond, Va.: John Knox Press, 1972), p. 145

36. Richard V. Pierard and Robert D. Linder

The civil religion reading of American history with its emphasis on special providence and the chosen nation has done untold mischief, as it served first to justify the destruction of the indigenous Indian culture and then foreign intervention, war and the imposition of American values, institutions and commercial enterprises on other peoples.

Civil Religion and the Presidency (Grand Rapids, Mich.: Zondervan, 1988), p. 297

CONSTITUTIONS

37. Alabama Constitution

No money raised for the support of the public schools shall be appropriated to or used for the support of any sectarian or denominational school.

Article XIV, Education (similar provisions are found in twenty-four other state constitutions.
All of the state constitutional provisions on religious liberty
and church-state relations may be found in
Religious Liberty and State Constitutions, ed. Edd Doerr and Albert J. Menendez
(Amherst, N.Y.: Prometheus Books, 1993).

38. Alaska Constitution

No sectarian instruction shall be imparted in any school or State educational institution that may be established under this Constitution, and no religious or political test or qualification shall ever be required as a condition of admission into any public educational institution of the State, as teacher, student, or pupil; but the liberty of conscience hereby secured shall not be so construed as to justify practices or conduct inconsistent with the good order, peace, morality, or safety of the State, or with the rights of others.

Article XI, Education, Section 7 (similar provisions are found in fifteen other state constitutions).

39. Arizona Constitution

No religious qualification shall be required for any public office or employment, nor shall any person be incompetent as a witness or juror in consequence of his opinion on matters of religion, nor be questioned touching his religious belief in any court of justice to affect the weight of his testimony.

Article 2, Declaration of Rights, Section 12
(similar provisions are found in seventeen other state constitutions).

40. Australia Constitution, Section 116

The Commonwealth shall not make any law for establishing any religion, or for imposing any religious observance, or for prohibiting the free exercise of any religion, and no religious test shall be required as a qualification for any office or public trust under the Commonwealth.

41. Justice Harry Blackmun

The Free Exercise Clause at the very least was designed to guarantee freedom of conscience by prohibiting any degree of compulsion in matters of belief. It was offended by a burden on one's religion.

The Establishment Clause can be understood as designed in part to ensure that the advancement of religion comes only from the voluntary efforts of its proponents and not from support by the state. Religious groups are to prosper or perish on the intrinsic merit and attraction of their beliefs and practices.

Address at National Archives, Washington, D.C., June 23, 1987.

42. Simón Bolívar

In a political constitution no religion should be prescribed, because, according to the best doctrines on fundamental laws, these are the guarantees of political and civil rights, and, as religion does not pertain to either of these rights, it is of an indefinable nature in the social order and belongs to the moral and intellectual. Religion governs man in his home, in his office, within himself; it alone has the right to examine his intimate conscience. Laws, on the contrary, look on the surface of things; they do not govern except outside the house of the citizen. Applying these considerations, can a State govern the consciences of its subjects, watch over the fulfillment of religious laws, and reward or punish, when the tribunals are in Heaven and when God is the judge? The Inquisition alone would be capable of replacing such courts in this world. Shall the Inquisition return with its fiery torches? Religion is the law of the conscience. All law over it annuls it, for by imposing necessity for duty, there is destroyed the merit of faith which is the basis of religion. The sacred precepts and dogmas are useful, luminous, and of metaphysical evidence; all of us ought to profess them, but this is a moral and not a political duty.

Proyecto de Constitución para la Republica de Bolivia y Discurso del Libertador, Buenos Aires, 1826.
Bolívar's unheeded plea for church-state separation in the Bolivian constitution.

43. Constitution of Brazil, 1946

Freedom of conscience and belief is inviolable, and the free exercise of religious sects is assured, as long as they are not contrary to public order or good morals. Religious associations shall acquire juridical personality according to civil law. No one shall be deprived of his rights by reason of religious, philosophic, or political convictions. . . . Without restraint of the ones favored, religious ministration to the Armed Forces shall be offered by a Brazilian . . . ; cemeteries shall be secular in character and shall be administered by the municipal authority. All religious confessions shall be permitted to practice their rite therein. Religious associations may maintain private cemeteries, according to law. . . . Religious instruction shall be a part of the teaching schedule of public schools, matriculation therein shall be optional, and the instruction shall be provided in accordance with the religious confession of the pupil.

44. Constitution of Colombia, 1853

[Guaranteed to all Colombians is] the free profession, public or private, of their religion, providing it does not disturb the public peace, offend pure morals, nor impede the exercise of any other religion.

The first act of church-state separation in Latin America, the 1853
Constitution also barred forced contributions for the support of any religion.

45. Georgia State Constitution

No person within this state shall upon any pretence, be deprived of the inestimable privilege of worshipping God, in a manner agreeable to his own conscience, nor be compelled to attend any place of worship, contrary to his own faith and judgment, nor shall he ever be obligated to pay tithes, taxes, or any other rate, for the building or repairing of any place of worship, or for the maintenance of any minister or ministry, contrary to what he believes to be right, or hath voluntarily engaged to do. No one religious society shall ever be established in this state in preference to another, nor shall any person be denied the enjoyment of any civil right merely on account of his religious principles.

1798

46. Hawaii Constitution

No law shall be enacted respecting an establishment of religion or prohibiting the free exercise thereof. . . .

Article I, Bill of Rights, Section 3 (similar provisions are found in thirty-four other state constitutions).

47. Illinois Constitution

Neither the general assembly nor any county, city, town, township, school district or other public corporation shall ever make any appropriation or pay from any public fund whatever, anything in aid of any church or sectarian purpose, or to help support or sustain any school, academy, seminary, college, university or other literary or scientific institution, controlled by any church or sectarian denomination whatever; nor shall any grant or donation of land, money or other personal property ever be made by the State or any such public corporation to any church or for any sectarian purpose.

48. Indiana Constitution

No preference shall be given, by law, to any creed, religious society, or mode of worship; and no man shall be compelled to attend, erect, or support, any place of worship, or to maintain any ministry, against his consent.

Article I, Bill of Rights, Section 4 (similar provisions are found in twenty-eight other state constitutions).

49. Japan, 1947 Constitution, Article 20

Freedom of religion is guaranteed to all. No religious organizations shall receive any privileges from the state nor exercise any political authority. No person shall be compelled to take part in any religious act, celebration, rite or practice. The state and its organs shall refrain from religious education or any other religious activity.

50. Kentucky Constitution, 1792

That all men shall have a natural and indefeasible right to worship Almighty God according to the dictates of their own consciences; that no man of right can be compelled to attend, erect, or support any place of worship, or to maintain any ministry against his consent; that no human authority can in any case whatever control or interfere with the rights of conscience; and that no preference shall ever be given by law to any religious societies or modes of worship.

    That the civil rights, privileges, or capacities of any citizen shall in no ways be diminished or enlarged on account of his religion.

Article XII, Sections 3 and 4

51. New Hampshire Constitution

Every individual has a natural and unalienable right to worship God according to the dictates of his own conscience, and reason; and no subject shall be hurt, molested or restrained, in his person, liberty, or estate, for worshipping God in the manner and season most agreeable to the dictates of his own conscience, or for his religious profession, sentiments, or persuasion; provided he doth not disturb the public peace or disturb others in their religious worship.

Bill of Rights, 5th. (similar provisions are found in forty-five other state constitutions).

52. New Mexico Constitution

No religious test should ever be required as a condition of admission to the public schools or any educational institution of this state, either as a teacher or student, and no teacher or student of such school or institution shall ever be required to attend or participate in any religious service whatsoever.

Article XII, Section 9

53. New York State Constitution

And whereas, We are required by the benevolent principles of rational liberty, not only to expel civil tyranny, but also to guard against that spiritual oppression and intolerance . . . the free exercise and enjoyment of religious profession and worship, without discrimination or preference, shall forever hereafter be allowed within this state to all mankind.

1777

54. ———

The free exercise and enjoyment of religious professions and worship, without discrimination or preference, shall forever be allowed in this state to all mankind; and no person shall be rendered incompetent to be a witness on account of his opinions on matters of religious belief; but the liberty of conscience hereby secured shall not be so construed as to excuse acts of licentiousness, or justify practices inconsistent with the peace or safety of the state.

Article I, Section 3

Neither the state nor any subdivision thereof shall use its property or credit or any public money, or authorize or permit to be used, directly or indirectly, in aid or maintenance, other than for examination or inspection, of any school or institution of learning wholly or in part under the control or direction of any religious denomination, or in which any denominational tenet or doctrine is taught, but the legislature may provide for the transportation of children to and from any school or institution of learning.

Article XI, Section 3 adopted in 1894.
(In 1967 a constitutional convention sought to delete Article XI, Section 3,
which led to 72 percent to 28 percent voter rejection of entire revised constitution.
[See Edd Doerr, The Conspiracy that Failed (Washington, D.C.: Americans United, 1968).])

55. Pennsylvania Constitution

That all persons living in this province who confess and acknowledge the one almighty and eternal God to be the creator, upholder, and ruler of the world, and that hold themselves obliged in conscience to live peaceably and justly in civil society, shall in no ways be molested or prejudiced for their religious persuasion

or practice in matters of faith and worship, nor shall they be compelled at any
time to frequent or maintain any religious worship, place, or ministry whatever.

Pennsylvania Code of 1682, Section 35, written by William Penn.

56. Puerto Rico Constitution

The dignity of the human being is inviolable. All men are equal before the law.
No discrimination shall be made on account of race, color, sex, birth, social
origin or condition, or political or religious ideas.

Article II, Section 1

No law shall be made respecting an establishment of religion or prohibiting the
free exercise thereof. There shall be complete separation of church and state.

Article II, Section 3

... There shall be a system of free and wholly non-sectarian public education.
Instruction in the elementary and secondary schools shall be free and shall be compulsory in the elementary schools to the extent permitted by the facilities of the
state. No public property or public fund shall be used for the support of schools or
educational institutions other than those of the state.

Article II, Section 5,
adopted by convention, approved by voters, and approved by U.S. Congress, 1952.

57. United States Constitution

Congress shall make no law respecting an establishment of religion, or prohibiting the free exercise thereof; or abridging the freedom of speech, or of the
press; or the right of the people peaceably to assemble, and to petition the Government for a redress of grievances.

Amendment I. Ratified December, 1791.

58. Wisconsin Constitution

No religious tests shall ever be required as a qualification for any office of public
trust under the state, and no person shall be rendered incompetent to give evidence in any court of law or equity in consequence of his opinions on the subject of religion.

Article I, Bill of Rights, Section 19 (similar provisions are found in thirty other state constitutions).

59. Wyoming Constitution

Appropriations for religion prohibited. No money of the state shall ever be given or appropriated to any sectarian or religious society or institution.

Article I, Declaration of Rights, Section 19
(similar provisions are found in forty-one other state constitutions).

60. William Butler Yeats

Once you attempt legislation upon religious grounds, you open the way for every kind of intolerance and religious persecution.

Remarks on the adoption of the Irish Constitution of 1937.

CREATIONISM

61. Central Conference of American Rabbis on Creationism in School Textbooks

Whereas the principles and concepts of biological evolution are basic to understanding science; and

Whereas students who are not taught these principles, or who hear "creationism" presented as a scientific alternative, will not be receiving an education based on modern scientific knowledge; and

Whereas these students' ignorance about evolution will seriously undermine their understanding of the world and the natural laws governing it, and their introduction to other explanations described as "scientific" will give them false ideas about scientific methods and criteria;

Therefore be it resolved that the Central Conference of American Rabbis commend the Texas State Board of Education for affirming the constitutional separation of Church and State, and the principle that no group, no matter how large or small, may use the organs of government, of which the public schools are among the most conspicuous and influential, to foist its religious beliefs on others;

Be it further resolved that we call upon publishers of science textbooks to reject those texts that clearly distort the integrity of science and to treat other explanations of human origins for just what they are—beyond the realm of science;

Be it further resolved that we call upon science teachers and local school authorities in all states to demand quality textbooks that are based on modern, scientific knowledge and that exclude "scientific" creationism;

Be it further resolved that we call upon parents and other citizens concerned about the quality of science education in the public schools to urge their Boards of Education, publishers, and science teachers to implement these needed reforms.

Ninety-fifth Annual Convention, 1984

62. Episcopal Church Resolution on Evolution and Creationism

Whereas, the state legislatures of several states have recently passed so-called "balanced treatment" laws requiring the teaching of "Creation-science" whenever evolutionary models are taught; and

Whereas, in many other states political pressures are developing for such "balanced treatment" laws; and

Whereas, the terms "Creationism" and "Creation-science" as understood in these laws do not refer simply to the affirmation that God created the Earth and Heavens and everything in them, but specify certain methods and timing of the creative acts, and impose limits on these acts which are neither scriptural nor accepted by many Christians; and

Whereas, the dogma of "Creationism" and "Creation-science" as understood in the above context has been discredited by scientific and theological studies and rejected in the statements of many church leaders; and

Whereas, "Creationism" and "Creation-science" is not limited to just the origin of life, but intends to monitor public school courses, such as biology, life science, anthropology, sociology, and often also English, physics, chemistry, world history, philosophy, and social studies; therefore be it

Resolved, that the 67th General Convention affirm the glorious ability of God to create in any manner, whether men understand it or not, and in this affirmation reject the limited insight and rigid dogmatism of the "Creationist" movement, and be it further

Resolved, that we affirm our support of the sciences and educators and of the Church and theologians in their search for truth in this Creation that God has given and intrusted to us; and be it further

Resolved, that the Presiding Bishop appoint a Committee to organize Episcopalians and to cooperate with all Episcopalians to encourage actively their state legislators not to be persuaded by arguments and pressures of the "Creationists" into legislating any form of "balanced treatment" laws or any law requiring the teaching of "Creation-science."

Sixty-seventh General Convention, 1982

63. Langdon Gilkey

There can be no healthy, creative or significant religious faith in a modern society unless the forms of that faith are free. A politically enforced or supported religious faith becomes corrupt, dead and oppressive, encouraging inevitably in reaction a deep personal distaste and moral disdain at such spiritual imperialism. Enforced religion breeds precisely what it most fears: rebellion against religion, cynicism about religion, skepticism about its claims, and, as a consequence, indifference at best and outright antipathy at worst. The First Amendment is important not only to guarantee the rights of alternative religions and of non-religious persons in society; it is also important in setting the only possible legal and social conditions for the creative health of serious religion itself.

Creationism on Trial (Minneapolis, Minn.: Winston-Seabury, 1985)

64. Martha Kegel, ACLU Activist

The proponents of scientific creationism are trying to sneak religion into the public schools. . . . The fact remains that creationism is a Bible story and teaching it as science in public schools violates the rights of religious minorities.

Interview, Hammond (LA) Daily Star (December 3, 1981)

65. Eugenie C. Scott

Religious opposition to evolution propels antievolutionists, although antievolutionists pay lip service to supposed scientific problems with evolution. What motivates them to battle its teaching is apprehension over the implications of evolution for religion.

"Antievolution and Creationism in the United States," Annual Review of Anthropology 26 (1997): 264.
Scott is executive director of the National Center for Science Education.

66. Unitarian Universalist Association

Whereas, the constitutional principles of religious liberty and the separation of church and state that safeguards liberty, and the ideal of a pluralistic society are under increasing attack in the Congress of the United States, in state legislatures, and in some sectors of the communications media by a combination of sectarian and secular special interests;

Be it resolved: That the 1982 General Assembly of UUA reaffirms its support for these principles and urges the Board of Trustees and President of the Association, member societies, and Unitarian Universalists in the United States to: Uphold religious neutrality in public education, oppose all government mandated or sponsored prayers, devotional observances, and religious indoctrination in public schools; and oppose efforts to compromise the integrity of public school teaching by the introduction of sectarian religious doctrines, such as "scientific creationism," and by exclusion of educational materials on sectarian grounds. . . .

Resolution Opposing "Scientific Creationism." Passed at the 21st Annual General Assembly, 1982.

67. United Presbyterian Church in the U.S.A.

Whereas, The Program Agency of the United Presbyterian Church in the USA notes with concern a concerted effort to introduce legislation and other means for the adoption of a public school curriculum variously known as "Creationism" or "Creation Science,"

Whereas, over several years, fundamentalist church leadership, resourced by the Creation Science Research Center and the Institute for Creation Research, has prepared legislation for a number of states calling for "balanced treatment" for "creation-science" and "evolution-science," requiring that wherever one is taught the other must be granted a comparable presentation in the classroom;

Whereas, this issue represents a new situation, there are General Assembly policies on Church and State and Public Education which guide us to assert once again that the state cannot legislate the establishment of religion in the public domain;

Whereas, the dispute is not really over biology or faith, but is essentially about Biblical interpretation, particularly over two irreconcilable viewpoints regarding the characteristics of Biblical literature and the nature of Biblical authority;

Therefore, the Program Agency recommends to the 194th General Assembly (1982) the adoption of the following affirmation:

Affirms that, despite efforts to establish "creationism" or "creation-science" as a valid science, it is teaching based upon a particular religious dogma as agreed by the court (*McLean* v. *Arkansas Board of Education*);

Affirms that, the imposition of a fundamentalist viewpoint about the interpretation of Biblical literature—where every word is taken with uniform literalness and becomes an absolute authority on all matters, whether moral, religious, political, historical or scientific—is in conflict with the perspective on Biblical interpretation characteristically maintained by Biblical scholars and theological schools in the mainstream of Protestantism, Roman Catholicism and Judaism. Such scholars find that the scientific theory of evolution does not conflict with their interpretation of the origins of life found in Biblical literature;

Affirms that, academic freedom of both teachers and students is being further limited by the impositions of the campaign most notably in the modification of textbooks which limits the teaching about evolution but also by the threats to the professional authority and freedom of teachers to teach and students to learn;

Affirms that, required teaching of such a view constitutes an establishment of religion and a violation of the separation of church and state, as provided in the First Amendment to the Constitution and laws of the United States;

Affirms that, exposure to the Genesis account is best sought through the teaching about religion, history, social studies and literature, provinces other than the discipline of natural science; and

Calls upon Presbyterians, and upon legislators and school board members, to resist all efforts to establish any requirements upon teachers and schools to teach "creationism" or "creation science."

Evolution and Creationism. Adopted by the General Assembly, 1982.

ECCLESIASTICAL POWER

68. J. B. Bury, Irish Historian

[T]he ideal of progress, freedom of thought, and the decline of ecclesiastical power go together.

A History of Freedom of Thought, 1913

69. James Connoly, Irish Labor Leader

Whenever the clergy succeeded in conquering political power in any country, the result has been disastrous to the interests of religion and inimical to the progress of humanity.

George Seldes, *The Great Quotations* (New York: Lyle Stuart, 1960), p. 166

70. Joseph Martin Dawson, first Executive Director, Baptist Joint Committee

It is a fixed American opinion that whenever and wherever churches have been able to invoke the power of the state in their behalf, the effects have been disastrous to moral character, to spiritual ideals and the good order of society.

Separate Church and State Now (New York: Richard R. Smith, 1948), p. 13

71. Daniel Defoe

And of all the plagues with which mankind are cursed ecclesiastic tyranny's the worst.

The True-Born Englishman, Part 2

72. Justice William O. Douglas

Christianity has sufficient inner strength to survive and flourish on its own. It does not need state subsidies, nor state privileges, nor state prestige. The more it obtains state support, the greater it curtails human freedom.

The Bible and the Schools (New York: Doubleday, 1966), p. 10

73. Rev. James Evans, Colgate Rochester Divinity School

Whenever in history the church has assumed the power of the state, or the state has assumed the power of the church, it has been to the detriment of both.

Rochester Democrat & Chronicle, February 1, 1986

74. Razelle Frankel

A country dominated by televangelism would be unrecognizable to the Founding Fathers, who envisioned religion as personal and spiritual, not social and political. No particular variety of religion was intended to control the political agenda, to set the community's moral tone or to judge who are the true believers and members of our society. But this is precisely the objective of the electric church.

Televangelism (Carbondale: Southern Illinois University Press, 1987)

75. Zelotes Fuller

The past history of the Christian Church should be a solemn warning to us never to permit an alliance to be formed between the priesthood and the civil magistracy—between Church and State powers.

Blau, *Cornerstones of Religious Freedom in America* (Boston: Beacon Press, 1949), p. 137

76. Winfred E. Garrison

The totalitarian church-state is always intolerant. Staking its very existence upon the hypothesis that everybody within its jurisdiction must conform to the approved patterns, it uses whatever means seem to be necessary to secure that end.

Intolerance (New York: Round Table Press, 1934), p. 124

77. Robert Hall

Turn a Christian society into an Established church and it is no longer a voluntary assembly for the worship of God; it is a powerful corporation, full of such sentiments and passions as usually distinguish those bodies—a dread of innovation, an attachment to abuses, a propensity to tyranny and oppression.

Quoted in James Barr, *The United Free Church of Scotland* (London: Allenson, 1934), pp. 173–74.

78. President Thomas Jefferson

The clergy, by getting themselves established by law and ingrafted into the machine of government, have been a very formidable engine against the civil and religious rights of man.

Saul K. Padover, *Thomas Jefferson on Democracy* (New York: New American Library, 1946), p. 165

79. Rev. Martin Luther King Jr.

The church must be reminded that it is not the master or the servant of the state, but rather the conscience of the state. It must be the guide and the critic of the state, and never its tool.

Strength to Love (New York: Harper & Row, 1963)

80. William E. H. Lecky

Almost all Europe, for many centuries, was inundated with blood, which was shed at the direct instigation or with the full approval of the ecclesiastical authorities.

History of the Rise and Influence of the Spirit of Rationalism in Europe
(New York: Appleton, 1866), vol. 2, p. 32

81. President James Madison

Besides the danger of a direct mixture of religion and civil government, there is an evil which ought to be guarded against in the indefinite accumulation of property from the capacity of holding it in perpetuity by ecclesiastical corporations.

The establishment of the chaplainship in Congress is a palpable violation of equal rights as well as of Constitutional principles.

The danger of silent accumulations and encroachments by ecclesiastical bodies has not sufficiently engaged attention in the U.S.

From the "Detached Memoranda." See Elizabeth Fleet, "Madison's
Detached Memoranda," *William and Mary Quarterly* 3 (1946): 554–62.

82. ———

Ecclesiastical establishments tend to great ignorance and corruption, all of which facilitate the execution of mischievous projects.

Letter to Bradford, January 1774

83. George A. Reid

Probably in all history there is no instance of a society in which ecclesiastical power was dominant which was not at once stagnant, corrupt and brutal.

George Seldes, *The Great Quotations* (New York: Lyle Stuart, 1967)

84. Justice Joseph Story

It was under a solemn consciousness of the dangers from ecclesiastical ambition, the bigotry of spiritual pride, and the intolerance of sects . . . that it was deemed advisable to exclude from the national government all power to act upon the subject.

Quoted in M. Searle Bates, *Religious Liberty: An Inquiry*,
(New York: International Missionary Council, 1945), p. 90.

85. Rabbi Sherwin T. Wine, Cofounder of Americans for Religious Liberty

For many years freedom struggled with an idea. It was a powerful idea, so powerful that many people tortured and killed others to make it real. The devotees of this idea believed, with all their heart, that no nation could long survive without the help of God. Nor would it endure without the guidance of his chosen ministers. State and religion must be one, just as child and parent are one, just as subject and master are one.

Two hundred years ago the forces of freedom challenged the idea. The children of the new enlightenment rose up to defy the tyranny of arrogant clergy and the censorship of pious bureaucrats. They boldly proclaimed that the state must be free from religious coercion and that religion must be free from state control. All individuals have the right to pursue the dictates of their own conscience. All citizens even have the right not to be religious at all.

Service, Birmingham Temple, Farmington Hills, Mich. (October 21, 1988)

EQUAL ACCESS ACT OF 1984

86. Rep. Don Edwards

Having lost the prayer amendment in the Senate—and lost badly—its proponents are attempting to come in through the back door, using the soothing, ostensibly neutral language of equal access.

Remarks, U.S. House of Representatives (May 15, 1984)

FREEDOM OF CONSCIENCE

87. President John Adams

We should begin by setting conscience free. When all men of all religions . . . shall enjoy equal liberty, property, and an equal chance for honors and power . . . we may expect that improvements will be made in the human character and the state of society.

Letter to Dr. Price, April 8, 1785

88. Hans Denk, Sixteenth-century Swiss Anabaptist

The state authorities have no place in the church of God, no right to control and persecute the conscience.

Written in the 1580s.

89. James II, King of England

It is and has of long time been our constant sense and opinion that conscience ought not to be constrained, nor people forced in matters of religion.

Declaration of Indulgence, October 1687.
Henry Kamen, *The Rise of Toleration* (New York: McGraw-Hill, 1967), p. 209.

90. President Thomas Jefferson

It behooves every man who values liberty of conscience for himself, to resist invasions of it in the case of others.

Letter to Benjamin Rush, April 21, 1803.

91. David Little

By means of the Lockean and Baptist connections, the single most important and determinative contribution [Roger] Williams made to the articulation of the principles of religious freedom and separation of church and state in late-eighteenth-century America was his doctrine of the free conscience, and the web of beliefs surrounding that doctrine.

There can be no doubt that the concept of the conscience and its right to free exercise lay at the heart of the thinking of individuals like Jefferson and Madison, thinking that finally produced the religion clauses of the First Amendment.

"The Reformed Tradition," from the *First Freedom: Religion and the Bill of Rights*, edited by James E. Wood Jr. (Waco, Tex.: J. M. Dawson Institute of Church-State Studies, 1990), p. 21.

92. President James Madison

Conscience is the most sacred of all property.

National Gazette (March 29, 1792)

93. John Milton

The liberty of conscience, which above all things ought to be to all men dearest and most precious . . .

The Ready and Easy Way to Establish a Free Commonwealth (New Haven: Yale University Press, 1915), p. 36

94. ———

Give me the liberty to know, to utter, and to argue freely according to conscience, above all other liberties.

Areopagitica, 1644

95. President Theodore Roosevelt

To discriminate against a thoroughly upright citizen because he belongs to some particular church, or because, like Abraham Lincoln, he has not avowed his allegiance to any church, is an outrage against that liberty of conscience which is one of the foundations of American life.

Letter to J. C. Martin, November 9, 1908.

96. President John Tyler

Let it be henceforth proclaimed to the world that man's conscience was created free; that he is no longer accountable to his fellow man for his religious opinions, being responsible therefore only to his God.

Caroline Thomas Harnsberger, *Treasury of Presidential Quotations* (Chicago: Follett, 1964), p. 38

LAW AND RELIGION

97. *America*, Jesuit Weekly

In a pluralistic society a fundamental assumption of public policy is the recognition that everything immoral need not be declared illegal. The public morality that is expressed in law reflects a consensus derived from public debate. . . . Social realities as well as religious principles must be taken into account in judging the wisdom of any legislation. Citizens who come to different conclusions are not necessarily immoral or unChristian. The tendency to so brand one's political opponents suggests a kind of moral fascism.

Editorial, September 13, 1980

98. Bishop James Armstrong, United Methodist Church

In a pluralistic society, no group, no matter how numerous or powerful, has a right to prescribe a set of beliefs or a code of ethics for all. Our individual and institutional efforts dare not betray the spirit of the religion we confess or subvert the Bill of Rights.

Address, Phoenix, Ariz., February 4, 1975

99. Jeremy Bentham

No power of government ought to be employed in the endeavor to establish any system or article of belief on the subject of religion.

Constitutional Code, George Seldes, *The Great Quotations*
(New York: Lyle Stuart, 1960), p. 813

100. Justice Harry Blackmun

The Free Exercise Clause at the very least was designed to guarantee freedom of conscience by prohibiting any degree of compulsion in matters of belief. It was offended by a burden on one's religion.

The Establishment Clause can be understood as designed in part to ensure that the advancement of religion comes only from the voluntary efforts of its proponents and not from support by the state. Religious groups are to prosper or perish on the intrinsic merit and attraction of their beliefs and practices.

Address at the National Archives, Washington, D.C., June 23, 1987.

101. Donald Boles

Judicial decisions and executive branch actions designed to erode the separation of church and state, by creating state-sanctioned orthodoxy, will undermine the foundation of all of the rights in our Bill of Rights and seriously weaken the fabric which has insured a maximum freedom for religious diversity.

Ironically, those religious fundamentalists who are agitating for national laws formalizing some of their religious beliefs are nourishing a beast that can turn and rend them. Should the major religions combine their strengths to create a divergent state of religious orthodoxy, fundamentalists will be placed in the position of a permanent and suppressed minority.

Religion and Public Education (fall 1984)

102. Irving Brant

On a full survey of the Supreme Court's decisions on religion and the criticisms of those decisions, a clear pattern emerges. The Court is working to protect the country against a breakdown of constitutional guarantees that would hurl the American people into a vortex of sectarian bitterness and strife. To do so it is obligated to call a halt to practices that range in effect from trivial harm to minor good. Popular dislike of these decisions is played upon by those who desire to break the barriers between church and state.

The Bill of Rights (Indianapolis: Bobbs-Merrill, 1965), p. 417.
Brant is the author of a six-volume biography of James Madison.

103. Sanford H. Cobb

It is the peculiar merit and glory of this American people that they were the first, and as yet the only one, among the nations to embody the principle of Religious Liberty in the fundamental law. Not toleration, but equality, puts all religions in the same relation to the law, under which there can be no preferences one before another. The only relation between the church and the state is that of mutual respect.

The Rise of Religious Liberty in America (New York: The Macmillan Company, 1902), p. 16

104. Cardinal Richard Cushing, Archbishop of Boston

Catholics do not need the support of civil law to be faithful to their religious convictions, and they do not seek to impose by law their moral views on other members of society.

Remarks, June 7, 1965, referring to the Supreme Court's *Griswold* decision.

105. Norman Dorsen

The continuing defense of civil liberties is indispensable if often thankless. Strong and determined opponents of human rights have always used the rhetoric of patriotism and practicality to subvert liberty and to dominate the weak, the unorthodox, and the despised. . . . As embodied in the Constitution and the Bill of Rights, these principles reflect a glorious tradition extending from the ancient world to modern times.

"Civil Liberties," from *Encyclopedia of the American Constitution*,
ed. Leonard W. Levy, Kenneth L. Karst, and Dennis J. Mahoney (New York: Macmillan, 1986), p. 379.

106. ———

Nonbelievers are protected by the religion clauses of the Constitution not because secular humanism is a religion, which it is not, but because when the government acts on the basis of religion it discriminates against those who do not "believe" in the governmentally favored manner.

William & Mary Law Review, vol. 26 (1986)

107. Justice William O. Douglas

The Free Exercise Clause protects the individual from any coercive measure that encourages him toward one faith or creed, discourages him from another, or makes it prudent or desirable for him to select one and embrace it.

The Bible and the Schools (New York: Doubleday, 1966), p. 10

108. Edwin S. Gaustad

Jefferson found in the religion phrases of the First Amendment no vague or fuzzy language to be bent or shaped or twisted as suited any Supreme Court Justice or White House incumbent. That amendment had built a wall, with the ecclesiastical estate on one side and the civil estate on the other.

Faith of Our Fathers (New York: Harper and Row, 1987), p. 46

109. John H. Laubach

A study of the Supreme Court rulings strongly suggests that the Court, in remaining faithful to the essence of the First Amendment, has not sought to insulate religious values from the arena of public policy formation. Essentially the Court held that public institutions may not be used to extract a confessional response from persons, nor to effect uniformity of doctrine or conscience, however minimal or subtle.

School Prayers: Congress, the Courts and the Public
(Washington, D.C.: Public Affairs Press, 1969), p. 151

110. Margaret Mead, Anthropologist

We will be a better country when each religious group can trust its members to obey the dictates of their own religious faith without assistance from the legal structure of the country.

Redbook magazine (February 1963)

111. Justice Lionel Murphy, High Court of Australia

The purpose of our [Australian] establishment clause is the same as that in the United States' Constitution. There does not seem to be any real doubt that if the establishment clause is construed in Australia as it is in the United States . . . then the challenged laws are unconstitutional. Section 116 of the Constitution does not assert or deny the value of religion (including religious teaching). It secures its free exercise, but denies that the Commonwealth cannot be concerned with religious teaching—that is entirely private. Section 116 recognises that an essential condition of religious liberty is that religion be unaided by the Commonwealth.

Dissenting opinion in *Attorney-General for Victoria v. the Commonwealth*, 33 A.L.R. 321 at 358 (1981)
from *Lionel Murphy: The Rule of Law*, ed. Jean and Richard Ely (Sydney: Akron Press, 1986).

112. Thomas Paine

Persecution is not an original feature in any religion; but is always the strongly marked feature of all law-religion, or religions established by law. Take away the law-establishment, and every religion re-assumes its original benignity.

The Rights of Man, 1791

113. John M. Swomley

When a church opposes the legalization or decriminalization of abortion or the sale of contraceptive birth control devices or the legal recognition of divorce, it demands more than a democratic secular state should grant. The state must not make something illegal because God or the Vicar of Christ forbids it. To ask the state to enforce God's will is to confuse church and state. It also confuses ethical obedience to one's faith with obedience derived from fear of the police.

The idea that individual personal morality or faith must be translated into public policy strikes at the heart of political and religious pluralism. In the United States we have come to believe that government is not the exclusive property of one faith, that government must be the protector of persons of every faith and of none.

From "Politics Centered Upon Abortion," *The Churchman* (April 1985).

114. U.S. District Judge Thomas A. Wiseman Jr.

Use of the mechanism of government to enforce momentary majoritarian morality upon which there is no real consensus, creates greater divisiveness in society, disrespect for law, and disrespect for the moral authority of the particular religion.

Address, Pulaski, Tenn., December 29, 1985

PAROCHIAID (GOVERNMENT AID TO SECTARIAN SCHOOLS)

115. Rev. E. Burdette Backus, Unitarian Minister

The founders of our nation deliberately entered upon the experiment of separating church and state. Because they saw the great evils of the union of the two they intentionally established a secular state, leaving the churches free to cultivate the religious life of the people. Our practice has not been entirely consistent with that principle, but on the whole we have been true to it and it has become woven into the warp and woof of our national life. It was freely predicted, when the experiment began, that it would be a failure, that a state could not exist on a secular basis. But those who so claimed have been proved false prophets by the course of our history, for we have grown great and powerful. One of the sources of our success has been the separation of church and state.

Under that policy we have developed a magnificent public school system. It has its defects as all human institutions do, but, by and large, it is the greatest single cultural achievement of our nation. It has done more to bring education to all the people than any other school system in the history of the world. It is one of the great bulwarks of our democracy.

"The 'Champaign Atheist' Trial" (Sermon, September 23, 1945),
in *Timely and Timeless: The Wisdom of E. Burdette Backus* (Amherst, N.Y.: Humanist Press, 1998).

116. President Bill Clinton

My administration has consistently opposed any action that seeks to provide public tax dollars in the form of vouchers to be used at private or religious schools. I do not believe that diverting funds to private providers is the answer to our educational challenges.

Letter to Americans for Religious Liberty, April 24, 1996

117. Peter W. Cookson Jr.

Any large-scale voucher plan will undermine public education and lead to a form of educational anarchy.

School Choice: The Struggle for the Soul of American Education
(New Haven: Yale University Press, 1994)

118. Monsignor Thomas J. Curry

There is simply no possibility that Catholic education can receive substantial public assistance and that the church can at the same time maintain complete control and direction of its schools. The reception of public monies must inevitably involve public supervision or control. . . .

The greatest danger for Catholic schools is not that they may fail to secure public assistance, but that in order to receive such aid they may secularize themselves piecemeal in the process. . . .

America, April 5, 1986

119. Sen. Sam J. Ervin Jr.

Government is contemptuous of true religion when it confiscates the taxes of Caesar to finance the things of God.

"Open Letter to President Reagan," *Congressional Record*, April 29, 1982.

120. Florence Flast, Vice-Chair, Committee for Public Education and Religious Liberty (PEARL)

Religious liberty in America means not only the right to pursue one's own beliefs, but freedom from compulsory taxation to foster the religious beliefs of others.

"Why Parochiaid Is a Threat to Public Education and Religious Liberty," statement issued June 12, 1972

121. ———

A proliferation of state-financed private and religious schools would greatly increase the tax burden on our citizenry. It would encourage racial, class and religious segregation, pitting one group against another in the political arena in bitter competition for the tax dollar. It would invite religious conflicts and the inequities of Southern style school segregation.

Ibid.

122. ———

The survival of free public education, the integrity of religious institutions, and the security of American democracy all demand an end to government financing of sectarian schools.

Ibid.

123. The Fleischmann Report

Civic tranquillity is best maintained by having the state remain apart from the sphere of religion and religious institutions.

New York, 1972

124. Marvin E. Frankel, U.S. District Judge

The wall of separation has been a treasure for the polyglot American family. The opponents of the principle—those who seek the clout of government to back their religious beliefs—base themselves on erroneous views of history and of true religious devotion. In a long, prudent perspective, it can be seen that they risk freedom of religion for themselves as well as others. This was understood by the framers of the Bill of Rights.

Faith and Freedom: Religious Liberty in America (New York: Hill and Wang, 1994), p. 21

125. President James Garfield

Next in importance to freedom and justice is popular education, without which neither justice nor freedom can be permanently maintained. Its interests are intrusted to the States and the voluntary action of the people. Whatever help the nation can justly afford should be generously given to aid the States in supporting common schools; but it would be unjust to our people and dangerous to our institutions to apply any portion of the revenues of the nation or of the States to the support of sectarian schools. The separation of Church and State in everything relating to taxation should be absolute.

Letter of acceptance of presidential nomination, July 12, 1880

126. Joanne Goldsmith, Executive Director, National Coalition for Public Education and Religious Liberty

The great majority of Americans firmly oppose the use of government funds to help finance religiously affiliated schools. . . . We hope that Congress will recognize that proposals for federal aid to sectarian schools embody a substantial and harmful departure from constitutional principle and tradition.

Testimony, U.S. House of Representatives, September 21, 1977

127. Al Gore, Vice President of the United States

Voucher proposals would drain precious resources from our public schools and would barely benefit the students who need help the most.

Address, National PTA, March 23, 1998

128. President Ulysses S. Grant

Encourage free schools and resolve that not one dollar appropriated for their support shall be apportioned to the support of any sectarian schools. Resolve that neither the state nor nation, nor both combined, shall support institutions of learning other than those sufficient to afford every child growing up in the land of opportunity of a good common school education, unmixed with sectarian, pagan, or atheistical dogmas. Leave the matter of religion to the family altar, the church and the private school supported entirely by private contributions. Keep the church and state forever separate.

Address to the Army of the Tennessee, Des Moines, Iowa, September 25, 1875

129. *The Living Church*, Episcopal Magazine

Christians who care enough about their faith to want it properly taught to their children in the course of their education should care enough to pay for it, however heavy the burden. . . . When any of our tax money is used, directly or indirectly, to subsidize any religious teaching without our consent, government is coercing us in this realm where coercion does not belong.

Editorial, April 21, 1974

130. *Miami Herald*

For good reason that has nothing to do with religious prejudice, the nation decided long ago that public funds should not be diverted to private schools.

Editorial, October 16, 1972

131. *New York Times*

We respect the right of parents to send their children to religious schools if they wish, but they should recognize that this is a voluntary choice on their part. The state has no obligation to further religious training in this way. In fact, it has an obligation to keep hands off.

Editorial, March 29, 1967

132. G. Bromley Oxnam, Methodist Bishop

If parents have the natural right to determine the education of their children, a privilege this nation gladly gives, it follows that parents who refuse the benefits of these splendid public educational opportunities should pay for such private education as they insist upon.

The Nation's Schools (March 1947)

133. President Theodore Roosevelt

Because we are unqualifiedly and without reservation against any system of denominational schools, maintained by the adherents of any creed with the help of state aid, therefore, we as strenuously insist that the public schools shall be free from sectarian influences, and above all, from any attitude of hostility to the adherents of any particular creed.

Quoted in Reuben Maury, *The Wars of the Godly*
(New York: Robert M. McBride & Company, 1928), p. 213.

134. ———

I hold that in this country there must be complete severance of Church and State; that public moneys shall not be used for the purpose of advancing any particular creed; and therefore that the public schools shall be nonsectarian and no public moneys appropriated for sectarian schools.

Address, Carnegie Hall, October 12, 1915

135. Elihu Root, U.S. Secretary of State under Theodore Roosevelt

It is not a question of religion, or of creed, or of party; it is a question of declaring and maintaining the great American principle of eternal separation between Church and State.

Statement Against the Use of Public Funds
for Sectarian Education by the State of New York, 1894

136. Alfred E. Smith, Governor of New York, Democratic Candidate for President, 1928

I believe in the support of the public school as one of the cornerstones of American liberty. I believe in the right of every parent to choose whether his child shall be educated in the public school or in a religious school supported by those of his own faith.

Atlantic Monthly (April 1927)

137. *Washington Post*

Public schools, controlled by public boards of education, maintained by public funds and open to all the public regardless of race or religion, have served this country magnificently well. They have been usefully supplemented by private schools, privately controlled and maintained, offering special forms of education and indoctrination to pupils with special needs and desires. It would be a misfortune to confuse the two, especially where religion is concerned. For a separation of church from state has been proved by history to be an indispensable condition alike for political liberty and for religious liberty. Let religious teaching remain within the province of homes and churches and private schools. Let secular education remain within the province of governments controlled by the people and open to all the winds of politics.

Editorial, June 21, 1969

138. ———

Americans have every right, of course, to seek for their children a religiously oriented education and to send their children to private schools which provide the sort of religious orientation they want. But they have no more right to ask the general public to pay for such schools—and for the religious instruction they provide—than to ask the general public to pay for the churches in which, happily, they are free to gather for prayer and for worship as they please.

The religious schools are organs of a church. The public schools are organs of a secular authority, the state. Would it not be wiser, as the founders of the Republic concluded, to keep church and state altogether separate?

Editorial, March 3, 1971

PLURALISM

139. Robert Baird

The freedom allowed in the United States to all sorts of inquiry and discussion necessarily leads to a diversity of opinion, which is seen not only in their being different denominations, but different opinions also in the same denomination.

Religion in America, 1856, p. 578

140. Lee Boothby

True religious freedom for a truly pluralistic society cannot exist when the state continues to support regulations that deny privileges to, or impose sanctions on, specific religious organizations or their members. Just as democracy has brought deregulation of the economic marketplace, religious freedom for a religiously pluralistic nation can only take place in a deregulated religious marketplace. . . .

Religious pluralism is not a problem simply to be coped with. Rather, it is a principle protected by international standards. Pluralism is not an aberration to be tolerated, but rather a right to be guaranteed. Those nations that have truly embraced religious pluralism and provided the full course of religious freedom have enjoyed both religious revival and reduction of internal tensions that otherwise exist as a result of such diversity.

"Pluralism: The Pathway to Peace," *Fides et Libertas* (1998): 60–61

141. Stephen L. Carter

Religious pluralism and equality—never mere toleration—should be essential parts of what makes American democracy special.

The Culture of Disbelief (New York: Basic Books, 1993), p. 21

142. Richard Cimino

Rather than spark interfaith conflict, American religious pluralism can defuse tension. With so many faith groups interacting in the public square, tolerance—if not always interfaith understanding—makes more sense than religious warfare.

Shopping for Faith: American Religion in the New Millennium
(San Francisco: Jossey-Bass Publishers, 1998), p. 188

143. Alan Dershowitz

At a time when ethnic and religious warfare is bloodying much of the world, Americans should count the blessings of the religious pluralism that has made their country so great and so stable. The Christian right wants to end all of this and bring religious warfare to our shores.

The Vanishing American Jew (Boston: Little, Brown and Company, 1996), p. 153

144. Norman Dorsen

We in the United States are pluralistic respecting ultimate beliefs. Profound values exist apart from a devotion to a god. Indeed, those who discriminate against nonbelievers flout the principle of religious tolerance that they often profess.

William and Mary Law Review, vol. 26 (1986)

145. Berton Dulce and Edward J. Richter

The election of a President of Catholic faith in 1960 gave a ringing stamp of recognition to pluralism as an indelible fact of national and political and social life.

Religion and the Presidency (New York: Macmillan Co., 1962), p. 216

146. Geraldine A. Ferraro, Democratic Candidate for Vice President, 1984

We are a religious nation because we do not have a state religion, because the government guarantees freedom of religion but has no role in religion, because not only do we tolerate our religious differences, we celebrate them.

Ferraro: My Story (New York: Bantam, 1985)

147. Al Gore, Vice President

The richness and diversity of our religious tradition throughout history is a spiritual resource long ignored by people of faith, who are often afraid to open their minds to teachings first offered outside their own system of belief.

Earth in the Balance (Boston: Houghton Mifflin Co., 1992)

148. President Thomas Jefferson

Difference of opinion is advantageous in religion. The several sects perform the office of a censor morum over each other.

Notes on Virginia (1782)

149. Barry A. Kosmin and Seymour P. Lachman

There are no guaranteed religious monopolies in the United States.

One Nation Under God: Religion in Contemporary American Society
(New York: Harmony Books, 1993), p. 142

150. Barry A. Kosmin and Seymour P. Lachman

Religion took very different directions in the United States. The new American nation encouraged people to exercise religious liberty and opposed favoritism for any particular church . . . The First Amendment encouraged exercise of religious beliefs without any interference from the state or state support.

Ibid., p. 278

151. President James Madison

Freedom arises from a multiplicity of sects, which pervades America, and which is the best and only security for religious liberty in any society.

Address to Virginia Constitutional Convention, June 12, 1788

152. William Martin

America has been remarkably favored by a wise constitutional policy of non-preferential protection for the free and responsible exercise of religion. For the good of the entire community of Americans, religious and secular alike, we should protect that policy against encroachments from whatever quarter.

With God on Our Side: The Rise of the Religious Right in America
(New York: Broadway Books, 1997), p. 385

153. Union of American Hebrew Congregations

The rise of extremism in some elements of American life . . . represents a clear and present danger to the tradition of American pluralism and a distortion of religious precepts in political life. We see these developments as a threat to the fabric of American life, to a democratic society, to Jewish values and to the security of American Jewry. The great strength of America lies in its pluralistic nature with its respect for diversity of viewpoints, whether liberal or conservative, Christian, Jewish, or any other.

Resolution adopted November 22, 1980.

RELIGION AND POLITICS

154. Robert S. Alley

Religious institutions have demonstrated an ability to manipulate the political system to their advantage.

Without a Prayer: Religious Expression in Public Schools
(Amherst, N.Y.: Prometheus Books, 1997), p. 60

155. *America*, Jesuit Weekly

In a pluralistic society a fundamental assumption of public policy is the recognition that everything immoral need not be declared illegal. The public morality that is expressed in law reflects a consensus derived from public debate. . . . Social realities as well as religious principles must be taken into account in judging the wisdom of any legislation. Citizens who come to different conclusions are not necessarily immoral or unChristian. The tendency to so brand one's political opponents suggests a kind of moral fascism.

Editorial, September 13, 1980

156. Anti-Defamation League of B'nai B'rith

We reject the notion that God and religion belong to any particular political party or candidate, or that advocates of the separation of church and state are intolerant or anti-religious.

Resolution, 1984 annual convention

157. *Baptist Standard*

Those quick to mix Christianity with the purely political are doing a disservice to religion.

Editorial, August 4, 1976

158. Joe L. Barnhart

The success of televangelists lies largely in their being parasites on family culture and morality. Far from providing a foundation for morality, they have gained for their religion a free ride on the back of the family culture that most Americans embrace.

Jim and Tammy (Amherst, N.Y.: Prometheus Books, 1990)

159. John C. Bennett

It is obvious that the churches in America should not use their members as political pressure groups to get special ecclesiastical privileges for themselves as against other religious bodies. They should not seek legislation, even if they can influence enough votes to get it, which interferes with the religious liberty of minorities and they should be thankful that the courts stand guard at this point.

Christians and the State (New York: Charles Scribner's Sons, 1958)

160. Cardinal Joseph Bernardin

[O]bviously in a religiously pluralistic society, getting consensus on what constitutes a public moral question is never easy. There is therefore an important distinction between moral principle and political/legal strategies.

"Religion and Politics: The Future Agenda," *Origins* 8 (November 1984): 321–66

161. Joseph L. Blau

Religion is too important an aspect of human life to be prostituted to politics, just as politics is too important a part of human life to be enslaved to religion.

"The Wall of Separation," *Union Seminary Quarterly Review* 38 (1984): 284

162. Irving Brant

In the present day, religious phraseology [in politics] is less an expression of feeling than a cloak to hide the absence of it.

The Bill of Rights, 1965, p. 424. Brant is the author of a six-volume biography of James Madison.

163. Monsignor Harry J. Byrne

It is a fact of life that American voters will never elect someone whom they view as politically subservient to a religious body.

America (December 7, 1986)

164. Walter H. Capps

Democracy and religious fundamentalism have never been good candidates for partnership because much of fundamentalism's deepest motivational energy involves instincts and impulses that run contrary, and are antithetical, to the spirit of democracy.

The New Religious Right: Piety, Patriotism and Politics
(Columbia: University of South Carolina Press, 1991).
Capps, a college professor, later served one term as a U.S. congressman from California.

165. Archbishop John Carroll, First U.S. Catholic Bishop

We are approaching to that happy term when in the appointment of men to offices of public trust, it will never be considered what religion does he profess, but only whether to be honest and able to fulfill it.

Letter, September 29, 1786

166. Jim Castelli, Journalist

Religion is good for American politics when it supports the civil religion; when it speaks out with civility and respect; when it accepts the principles of tolerance and pluralism; when it appeals to a shared sense of morality and not to religious authority or doctrine; when it reminds us that we are a community, not a collection of isolated individuals; when it reminds us that we are our brothers' and sisters' keepers.

Religion is bad for American politics when it undermines the civil religion: when it speaks of political matters with the certitude of faith in a pluralistic society in which faith cannot be used as a political standard; when it treats opponents as agents of Satan; when it weakens a sense of national community; when it violates the precept of the Virginia Statute for Religious Freedom which formed the basis for the First Amendment—the precept that any American should no more be treated any differently than any other American on the basis of his or her opinions about religion than on the basis of his or her opinions on literature or geometry. That is only common sense.

A Plea for Common Sense (New York: Harper & Row, 1988), p. 193

167. Central Conference of American Rabbis

Religion flourishes best when it is free of political alliances.

1962

168. Richard Cimino

Like a conservative chameleon, the religious right continues to reinvent itself.

Shopping for Faith: American Religion in the New Millennium
(San Francisco: Jossey-Bass Publishers, 1998), p. 136

169. James Connoly, Irish Labor Leader

Whenever the clergy succeeded in conquering political power in any country, the result has been disastrous to the interests of religion and inimical to the progress of humanity.

George Seldes, *The Great Quotations* (New York: Lyle Stuart, 1960), p. 166

170. "Cry for Renewal"

The almost total identification of the Religious Right with the new Republican majority in Washington is a dangerous liaison with political power. With the ascendancy and influence of the Christian Right in party circles, the religious critique of power has been replaced with the religious competition for power.

The "Cry for Renewal" statement, released on May 29, 1995, was signed by a number of Catholic, Protestant, and Eastern Orthodox leaders.

171. Mario Cuomo, Governor of New York

The American people need no course in philosophy or political science or church history to know that God should not be made into a celestial party chairman. To most of us, the manipulative invoking of religion to advance a politician or a party is frightening and divisive. The American people will tolerate religious leaders taking positions for or against candidates. . . . But the American people are leery about large religious organizations, powerful churches, or synagogue groups engaging in such activities—again, not as a matter of law or doctrine, but because our innate wisdom and democratic instinct teaches us these things are dangerous.

Address, University of Notre Dame, September 13, 1984

172. ——

Way down deep the American people are afraid of an entangling relationship between formal religions—or whose bodies of religious belief—and government. Apart from constitutional law and religious doctrine, there is a sense that tells us it's wrong to presume to speak for God or to claim God's sanction of our particular legislation and his rejection of all other positions. Most of us are offended when we see religion being trivialized by its appearance in political throw-away pamphlets.

Ibid.

173. Alan Dershowitz

Let there be no mistake about the ultimate goal of the Christian right: to turn the United States into a theocracy, ruled by Christian evangelicals. . . . As part of their theocratic program, the Christian right seeks to destroy the wall of separation between church and state and to establish Christianity as the official state religion.

The Vanishing American Jew (Boston: Little, Brown and Company, 1996), p. 154

174. Sara Diamond

Thanks to its sense of collective martyrdom, the Christian Right will surely continue to engage in conflict with the secular political culture. It is the Christian Right's dual nature as subculture and political faction that has made it such a potent force, and likely to adapt and endure in the years to come.

Not by Politics Alone: The Enduring Influence of the Christian Right
(New York: The Guilford Press, 1998), p. 238.

175. Russell H. Dilday Jr., President, Southwestern Baptist Theological Seminary

Individual Christians should be involved at every level of our democratic processes of government, but only to insure that personal freedom and justice are maintained, never to secure privileged support from the state or encourage its entanglement in religious affairs.

Church & State (October 1984)

176. James M. Dunn, Executive Director of the Baptist Joint Committee, 1981–1999

One of the most serious threats to civility in society is the medieval use and abuse of religion as weapon in polemical politics.

Truth with the Bark on It: The Wit and Wisdom of James M. Dunn
(Washington, D.C.: Baptist Joint Committee, n.d.), p. 19

177. Rep. Chet Edwards (D-Tex.)

The best way to ruin religion is to politicize it.

Address, U.S. House of Representatives, June 4, 1998

178. Episcopal Church

We insist that the use of religious radio and TV and local pulpits in support of particular candidates in the name of God distorts Christian truth and threatens American religious freedom.

Our refusal to entangle religion in partisan politics, and our wariness of contemporary movements that do, is rooted in a wise American tradition of avoiding the almost certain risk of political tyranny in the name of God.

House of Bishops, pastoral letter, October 8, 1980

179. Bruce L. Felknor

Religion, because of its capacity to rouse emotions and to generate zeal, can be a most dangerous ingredient in elections.

Address, National Conference of Christians and Jews, April 15, 1959.
Felknor was director of the Fair Campaign Practices Committee.

180. Geraldine A. Ferraro, Democratic Candidate for Vice President, 1984

Personal religious convictions have no place in political campaigns or in dictating public policy.

Ferraro: My Story (New York: Bantam, 1985), p. 211

181. ———

When I take my oath of office, I accept the charge of serving all the people of every faith, not just some of the people of my own faith. I also swear to uphold the Constitution of the United States, which guarantees freedom of religion. These are my public duties. And in carrying them out, I cannot, and I will not, seek to impose my own religious views on others.

Address in Scranton, Pa., October 24, 1984

182. President Millard Fillmore

I am tolerant of all creeds. Yet if any sect suffered itself to be used for political objects I would meet it by political opposition. In my view church and state should be separate, not only in form, but fact. Religion and politics should not be mingled.

Address during 1856 presidential election in Robert J. Rayback, *Millard Fillmore* (Buffalo, N.Y.: Henry Stewart, Inc., 1959), p. 407.

183. C. Welton Gaddy, Executive Director, Interfaith Alliance

We caution against the identification of religion with any one political point of view. Candidates are manipulating religion for their own purposes, and tragically making religion a ballot issue rather than a matter of personal faith.

Statement, February 24, 2000

184. George Gallup Jr. and Jim Castelli

American Catholics of all political persuasions do not want their bishops to appear even remotely to be telling them how to vote.

The American Catholic People (New York: Doubleday, 1987)

185. President James Garfield

In my judgment, while it is the duty of Congress to respect to the uttermost the conscientious convictions and religious scruples of every citizen . . . not any ecclesiastical organization can be safely permitted to usurp in the smallest degree the functions and powers of the national government.

Inaugural Address, March 4, 1881

186. Cardinal James Gibbons

A civilian ruler dabbling in religion is as reprehensible as a clergyman dabbling in politics. Both render themselves odious as well as ridiculous.

The Faith of Our Fathers, 1876

187. Sen. Barry M. Goldwater (R-Ariz.), Candidate for President

Being a conservative in America traditionally has meant that one holds a deep, abiding respect for the Constitution. We conservatives believe sincerely in the integrity of the Constitution. We treasure the freedom that document protects. . . .

By maintaining the separation of church and state, the United States has avoided the intolerance which has so divided the rest of the world with religious wars. Throughout our two hundred plus years, public policy debate has focused on political and economic issues, on which there can be compromise. . . .

The great decisions of government cannot be dictated by the concerns of religious factions. This was true in the days of Madison, and it is just as true today. We have succeeded for 205 years in keeping the affairs of state separate from the uncompromising idealism of religious groups and we mustn't stop now. To retreat from that separation would violate the principles of conservatism and the values upon which the framers built this democratic republic.

U.S. Senate Address, September 16, 1981

188. Al Gore, Vice President

I'm so troubled, always, when I see people who are sure that they know exactly what God's plan for the world is, what political party God belongs to, what God's ideology is, and what God's position on particular cases and controversies might be.

Statement to civil liberties and religious leaders July 14, 1994.

189. Rev. Billy Graham

I don't want to see religious bigotry in any form. It would disturb me if there was a wedding between the religious fundamentalists and the political right. The hard right has no interest in religion except to manipulate it.

Parade (February 1, 1981)

190. Louis Harris, Pollster

What is certain now is that many of the positions of the Religious Right are meeting with outright rejection from the American people. The Religious Right is a target of wrath for a sizable majority of the American people and a distinct political liability to those who embrace its cause.

Inside America (New York: Vintage Books, 1987)

191. James A. Haught

Religion, despite its universal message of compassion, can mix with politics, poverty, tribalism and social ferment to produce the destructive opposite of compassion. A great irony of the 1990s is that religion, supposedly a source of kindness and human concern, has taken the lead as the foremost contributing factor to hatred, war, and terrorism.

Holy Hatred: Religious Conflicts of the '90s (Amherst, N.Y.: Prometheus Books, 1995)

192. Rutherford B. Hayes

We all agree that neither the Government nor political parties ought to interfere with religious sects. It is equally true that religious sects ought not to interfere with the Government or with political parties. We believe that the cause of good government and the cause of religion suffer by all such interference.

Statement as governor of Ohio, 1875

193. Monsignor George G. Higgins

Americans do not want their President to use his high office to impose his own religious beliefs on the citizenry.

America (May 5, 1990): 454

194. President Herbert Hoover

Religion is a difficult matter to handle politically.

Quoted in Carl Sferazza Anthony, *America's First Families*
(New York: Touchstone Books, 2000), p. 217.

195. Molly Ivins, Texas Journalist

My ambivalence about fundamentalist Christians stems from their role in politics. I have always subscribed to the philosophy of Mr. Dooley, the great sage of

Chicago, who once inquired, "Is there, in all the history of human folly, a greater fool than a clergyman in politics?"

The politicization of fundamentalists, first seen in the mid-1970s in the form of the Moral Majority, has proceeded until now. These Shiite Baptists are simply running amok in politics.

Given the state of politics in this country, any reasonable person is entitled to conclude that politics could use an injection of the Good Book. But we are witnessing instead the very sort of divisive, doctrinal disputation—the insistence that all citizens behave according to the beliefs of some—that led our Founding Fathers to the doctrine of separation of church and state at the beginning of this nation.

I have recently noticed a number of misexplanations of separation of church and state being spread by fundamentalists. "It's not in the Constitution," they cry. Actually, it is, even though the words "separation of church and state" do not appear therein.

The Establishment Clause of the First Amendment is what separates church and state. The Founders were perfectly clear about what they were doing. It was put best by James Madison, in that magnificent eighteenth-century prose of which we are no longer capable: The purpose of the separation of church and state "is to keep forever from these shores the ceaseless strife that has soaked the soil of Europe in blood for centuries."

Fort Worth Star-Telegram (February 28, 1993)

196. Sen. Edward M. Kennedy (D-Mass.)

The foundation of our pluralism is that government will never determine which religion is right, and religion will not put its imprimatur on some politicians while damning others because of their political views.

Address, Liberty University, Lynchburg, Va., October 3, 1983

197. President John F. Kennedy

Whatever one's religion in his private life may be, for the officeholder, nothing takes precedence over his oath to uphold the Constitution and all its parts— including the First Amendment and the strict separation of church and state.

Interview, *Look* (March 3, 1959)

198. ———

I believe in an America where the separation of church and state is absolute—where no Catholic prelate would tell the President (should he be Catholic) how to act and no Protestant minister would tell his parishioners for whom to vote—where no church or church school is granted any public funds or political preference—and where no man is denied public office merely because his religion differs from the President who might appoint him or the people who might elect him.

I believe in an America that is officially neither Catholic, Protestant, nor Jewish—where no public official either requests or accepts instructions on public policy from the Pope, the National Council of Churches, or any other ecclesiastical source—where no religious body seeks to impose its will directly or indirectly upon the general populace or the public acts of its officials—and where religious liberty is so indivisible that an act against one church is treated as an act against all.

Address to the Ministerial Association of Greater Houston, September 12, 1960

199. ———

I believe in an America where religious intolerance will someday end—where all men and all churches are treated as equals—where every man has the same right to attend or not attend the church of his choice—where there is no Catholic vote, no anti-Catholic vote, no bloc voting of any kind—and where Catholics, Protestants, and Jews, at both the lay and pastoral level, will refrain from those attitudes of disdain and division which have so often marred their works in the past, and promote instead the American ideal of brotherhood.

Ibid.

200. ———

If my church attempted to influence me in a way which was improper or which affected adversely my responsibilities as a public servant sworn to uphold the Constitution, then I would reply to them that this was an improper action on their part. It was one to which I could not subscribe.

Press conference, Houston, Tex., September 12, 1960

201. ———

I hope that no American, considering the really critical issues facing this country, will waste his franchise and throw away his vote by voting either for me or against me solely on account of my religious affiliation.

Acceptance speech to the Democratic National Convention, Los Angeles, July 1960

202. Isaac Kramnick

The founders of this nation would regard the mixing of religion and politics in the ways now being engineered by the religious right as part of the problem of failing public morality, rather than as an answer.

The Godless Constitution, with R. Laurence Moore
(New York: W. W. Norton and Company, 1996), p. 153

203. ———

A religious party seems distinctly out of place in a country that made the elimination of an established church one of the first orders of national business.

Ibid., p. 160

204. ———

Whenever religion of any kind casts itself as the one true faith and starts trying to arrange public policy accordingly, people who believe that they have a stake in free institutions, whatever else might divide them politically, had better look out.

Ibid., p. 12

205. ———

If religious leaders attempt to pass legislation by arguing that it is God's will, if individuals run for office saying they do so with God's blessing, if members of a religious lobby endorse candidates for office only because they claim to be born-again Christians, they offend both American politics and the religious rules of this country set up to protect the free exercise of religion.

Ibid., p. 130

206. Seymour Martin Lipset

It is impossible to discuss the nature of political life in America without paying special attention to the influence of religious groups and values.

"Religion and Politics in American History," *Religion and Social Conflict,*
ed. Robert Lee and Martin E. Marty (New York: Oxford University Press, 1964), p. 109

207. Martin Marty

Fundamentalist movements often seek the restoration of a golden age . . . though a politics of nostaglia leads fundamentalists to wish for a return to a world they believe they have lost, that world—while rooted in historical reality—is also a mythical construction.

Politics, Religion and the Common Good (San Francisco: Jossey-Bass Publishers, 2000), p. 33

208. Mary McAleese

In Ireland, the work of reconciliation means that those churches which are embedded in the conflict must be unshackled from the chains which bind them to the language of conflict.

Love in Chaos: Spiritual Growth and the Search for Peace in Northern Ireland
(New York: Continuum Publishing Company, 1999), p. 112

209. ⸻

Reconciling political ambitions is not in itself the challenge facing the Christian churches. The challenge for the churches is to take the sectarian hatred out of the political discourse, to leave the politics and remove the poison.

Ibid., p. 81. Mary McAleese was elected president of the Republic of Ireland in 1997.

210. Rev. Richard P. McBrien

There is a crucial distinction to be made between the proclamation of views in the public forum and the harnessing of governmental power to impose those views on the general populace. Exclusive appeals to the Bible or the teaching authority of the Catholic Church are the weakest forms of public argument in a religiously pluralistic society.

Caesar's Coin: Religion and Politics in America (New York: Macmillan, 1987)

211. Eugene J. McCarthy

The Christian in politics should be judged by the standard of whether through his decisions and actions he has advanced the cause of justice. The Christian in politics should be distinguished by his alertness to protect and defend the rights of individuals, or religious institutions and other institutions, from violation by the state or by other institutions or persons. He has a very special obligation to keep the things of God separate from those of Caesar. The Christian in politics should shun the devices of the demagogue at all times, but especially in a time when anxiety is great, when tension is high, when uncertainty prevails, and emotion tends to be in the ascendancy.

"The Christian in Politics," *Commonweal* (October 1, 1954).
McCarthy served in the United States Congress as a representative and senator from Minnesota from 1949 to 1971. He was a candidate for president in 1968 and 1976. This article in the respected Catholic journal *Commonweal* was published during the heyday of McCarthyism—the political movement led by another McCarthy, Sen. Joseph McCarthy of Wisconsin.

212. Albert J. Menendez

The significance of the Kennedy Presidency as far as cultural pluralism is concerned is that it reaffirmed and revitalized the pluralist impulse and led to major accommodations between religious groups. JFK was a free man. By being free, he freed many Catholics and Protestants from the debilitating recriminations of the past.

John F. Kennedy: Catholic and Humanist (Amherst, N.Y.: Prometheus Books, 1979), p. 62

213. ————

It is the profound religious intolerance of the [Religious Right] movement which threatens to create a closed society, should it ever triumph, a society no longer open to a multiplicity of religious experiences, no longer welcoming or nurturing difference in religious belief and observance. If triumphant, it would obliterate two centuries of slow progress in extending the religious liberty guarantees of the Constitution to still more and more people. As a political force, it threatens to divide the nation's political life along religious lines, as did the now discredited European confessional parties of old. As a cultural force—and it is in the nebulous realm of culture where its influence is potentially greatest—it could engender a wasteland of ignorance, shallowness and superficiality unworthy of a great nation. It could very well be the death knell of a democratic way of life.

Three Voices of Extremism (Silver Spring, Md.: Americans for Religious Liberty, 1996), p. 119

214. Rev. John Meyendorff

The Christian faith and the values it implies will simply cease to be credible if it is reduced to political games and identified with electoral ambitions.

Editorial, *The Orthodox Church*, November 1980

215. James A. Michener, Novelist

I kept careful record of the impact of religion on the election in my county. The religious issue permeated every meeting I conducted. It influenced Republicans and Democrats alike. Ministers preached politics publicly and churches distributed the most vicious electioneering materials. Practically no one I met escaped the pressure of this overriding problem and both parties were ultimately forced to make their major calculations with the religious question a foremost consideration.

Report of the County Chairman (New York: Random House, 1961), pp. 106–107. Michener was chairman of Citizens for Kennedy in Bucks County, Pa., during the 1960 presidential campaign.

216. ———

Religious hatreds ought not to be propagated at all, but certainly not on a tax-exempt basis.

Ibid., p. 96. Michener discovered that most of the "avalanche of anti-Catholic literature" which deluged Bucks County came from tax-exempt religious publications and church newsletters.

217. Sen. Robert B. Morgan (D-N.C.)

Demagoguery from the pulpit is no different from demagoguery on the campaign trail. If anything, it is worse, because it clothes itself in self-righteousness.

Address, April 1980

218. *New York Times*

Americans ask piety in presidents, not displays of religious preference.

Editorial, January 31, 1984

219. Eleanor Roosevelt

The kind of propaganda that some of the religious groups, aided and abetted by the opposition, put forth in that campaign [1928] utterly disgusted me. If I needed anything to show me what prejudice can do to the intelligence of human beings that campaign was the best lesson I could have had.

Autobiography of Eleanor Roosevelt (New York: Harper & Row, 1961), p. 148

220. Rabbi David Saperstein

The intrusion of religious authority into politics undermines the unimpeded exercise of conscience which is so essential to a healthy democracy.

Quoted in *The Fundamentalist Phenomenon*, ed. by Norman J. Cohen
(Grand Rapids, Mich.: Eerdmans, 1990), p. 221.

221. Mark Silk

The public square has not been denuded of religion. To the contrary. Not only is American journalism fairly attentive to matters of faith, but it also approaches these in what can only be described as a proreligious posture.

Unsecular Media: Making News of Religion in America (Champaign: University of Illinois Press, 1995)

222. Paul D. Simmons

The incestuous marriage of religion and politics in our country seems to be the ruination of each.

Report from the Capital 40 (April 1985): 11

223. Alfred E. Smith, Governor of New York, Democratic Candidate for President, 1928

I can think of no greater disaster to this country than to have the voters of it divide upon religious lines.

Address, Oklahoma City, September 20, 1928

224. Sen. Arlen Specter (R-Pa.)

When Pat Robertson says there is no constitutional doctrine of separation between church and state, I say he is wrong. When Pat Buchanan calls for a holy war in our society, I say he is wrong. When Ralph Reed says a pro-choice Republican isn't qualified to be vice president, I say the Republican Party will not be blackmailed.

Statement announcing his candidacy for president, March 30, 1995

225. Statement by Four Religious Leaders

Religious freedom, based on the separation principle, has been the keystone of all our other freedoms. Freedom of religion has made possible our pluralistic society, with its capacity for negotiating and reconciling religious conflicts and differences that have so often plunged other societies into strife, misery, and bloodshed.

To create religious voting blocs on the American scene would be to discard these historic achievements—to invite a return to religious strife or oppression. It could bring us back to the conditions of colonial times, when theocratic rulers withheld religious liberty from the people.

Issued by Episcopal Bishop Paul Moore,
Dr. Arnold Olson of the Evangelical Free Church,
Rabbi Marc H. Tanenbaum of the American Jewish Committee,
and Rev. Joseph O'Hare, editor of *America*, on October 18, 1976.

226. A Statement on Religious Liberty in Relation to the 1960 National Campaign

We affirm that religious liberty is basic, both historically and philosophically, to all our liberties, and that religious and civil liberties are interdependent and indivisible.

We believe that it is the responsibility of the members of various religious organizations to oppose vigorously all attempts to make religious affiliation the basis of the voters' choice of candidates for public office. It is a vicious practice and repugnant to all honorable Americans to set class against class, race against race, and religion against religion.

The exclusion of members of any family of faith from public office on the basis of religious affiliation violates the fundamental conditions of a free democratic society, as expressed in the spirit of the Constitution.

The fact that a major religious group has so far never furnished the nation with a candidate who won election to a particular public office does not obligate the voters to elect a candidate of that faith to that office solely to demonstrate our devotion to democracy. This would establish a religious test for public office, contrary to the obvious intent of the Constitution. It would, furthermore, focus attention on a marginal qualification rather than on the essential qualities of personal integrity, leadership capacity, and policies relating to central issues.

No religious organization should seek to influence and dominate public officials for its own institutional advantage.

Excerpts from a statement issued September 12, 1960, by 107 leaders of the
Protestant, Catholic, Jewish, and Greek Orthodox faiths in response to religious bigotry and extremism
during the Kennedy-Nixon presidential election. Reprinted in full in Patricia Barrett's
Religious Liberty and the American Presidency (New York: Herder & Herder, 1963), pp. 152–60.

227. A Statement on Religious Liberty by American Catholic Laymen

We believe in the freedom of the religious conscience and in the Catholic's obligation to guarantee full freedom of belief and worship as a civil right. This obligation follows from basic Christian convictions about the dignity of the human person and the inviolability of the individual conscience. And we believe that Catholics have a special duty to work for the realization of the principle of freedom of religion in every nation, whether they are a minority or a majority of the citizens.

We deplore the denial of religious freedom in any land. We especially deplore this denial in countries where Catholics constitute a majority—even an overwhelming majority.

We believe that constitutional separation of church and state offers the best guarantee both of religious freedom and of civic peace. The principle of separation is part of our American heritage, and as citizens who are Catholics we value it as an integral part of our national life. Efforts which tend to undermine the principle of separation, whether they come from Catholics, Protestants, or Jews, should be resisted. . . .

Excerpts from a statement issued in October 1960. Barrett, Ibid., pp. 164–66

228. John M. Swomley

What is happening in present-day America is the rise of a radical religious right that attacks the secular state in order to make it a Christian nation, that attacks the secular public school system by insisting on Christian prayers in classes and at public school events and seeks control of local school boards by Christian Coalition sponsored or promoted candidates.

Unless the American people take this threat seriously, the radical religious right may eliminate some of our constitutional liberties and seriously change the face of American politics for the worse. The American dream could be transformed into a nightmare.

Religious Political Parties (Silver Spring, Md.: ARL, 1994), p. 62

229. President William Howard Taft

There is nothing so despicable as a secret society that is based upon religious prejudice and that will attempt to defeat a man because of his religious beliefs. Such a society is like a cockroach—it thrives in the dark. So do those who combine for such an end.

Address, December 20, 1914

230. Sen. Gulian C. Verplanck (D-N.Y.)

Whenever Congress or any other political body in this country meddles in affairs of religion, they must run counter . . . to the spirit of our free institutions securing equal religious rights.

You cannot make religion a party and an actor in the halls of human legislation without infinite and incalculable evil—evil to religion, evil to the state. You inflame the rancor of party politics by adding to it the fervor of religious zeal or that of sectarian fanaticism. Or else you do worse—you pollute and degrade religion by making her the handmaid of human power or the partisan of personal ambition.

Anson Phelps Stokes and Leo Pfeffer, *Church and State in the United States*, 1964, p. 505.

231. Kenneth D. Wald

Given the ambiguity of religious texts and teachings, the mixed historical record, and the empirical evidence, it would be foolhardy to assert that religious faith necessarily upholds democratic values.

Religion and Politics in the United States (New York: St. Martin's, 1986)

232. J. Brent Walker, Executive Director, Baptist Joint Committee on Public Affairs

When religion is dragged through the mud of a political campaign, no one should be surprised when it gets soiled.

Report from the Capital (March 7, 2000)

233. ———

Not only is the public square no longer naked, it is dressed to the nines. A healthful public discussion of religion has almost turned into a *de facto* religious test for public office and religion is often used as a cudgel for partisan advantage.

Ibid.

234. Jim Wallis

For several years now, the Religious Right has virtually controlled the national discussion of politics and morality with the help of the media, who have virtually ignored alternative voices.... The time has come to challenge the Religious Right and offer a deeper perspective. A clear, visible, public alternative is vitally needed today—one that lifts up another vision of the relationship between faith and politics.

Wallis, long-time editor of the liberal evangelical
Sojourners magazine, made this statement on May 29, 1995.

235. Sen. Lowell Weicker (R-Conn.)

The time has come to knock off this religion business in American politics. There's no end to the mischief that can occur. It is like putting nitroglycerine in a Waring blender.

Remarks, August 1984

236. Canon Edward West, Cathedral of St. John the Divine (Episcopal), New York City

The church's fundamental business is, and must be, religion. The church does badly in initiating legislation; its task is to inspire legislators. The omnicompetent state, whether theocratic or secular, is inevitably the enemy of human freedom. Whether it be the church handing over a heretic to the state for execution, or the state leaning on the church to enforce total conformity, the result is the same.

Churches on the Wrong Road (Washington, D.C.: Gateway Editions, 1986)

237. Clyde Wilcox

The failure of many Christian Right activists to support basic civil liberties is troubling. The core of the Christian Right agenda is not just about allowing conservative Christians to practice their religion and avoid public ridicule; it is about legislating morality.

Onward Christian Soldiers? The Religious Right in American Politics
(Boulder, Colo.: Westview Press, 1997), p. 147

238. Ellen Willis, Journalist

[A] democratic polity requires a secular state: one that does not fund or otherwise sponsor religious institutions and activities; that does not display religious symbols; that outlaws discrimination based on religious belief, whether by government or by private employers, landlords or proprietors—that does, in short, guarantee freedom from as well as freedom of religion. Furthermore, a genuinely democratic society requires a secular ethos: one that does not equate morality with religion, stigmatize atheists, defer to religious interests and aims over others or make religious belief an informal qualification for public office.

"Freedom from Religion: What's at Stake in Faith-Based Politics," *The Nation* (February 19, 2001)

239. James E. Wood Jr.

While there should be no question about the right of all Americans of whatever religious faith to participate in the political process, there is something quite ominous and threatening about any religious segment of this nation aiming to dominate a political party. . . . The injection of sectarian religion in the political process is not only divisive but does not bode well for the well-being of the Republican Party, a free and pluralistic society, or America's wide diversity of faiths.

"Religion and the U.S. Presidential Election of 1992,"
Journal of Church and State 34 (autumn 1992): 726, 728

240. Rep. James C. Wright Jr. (D-Tex.)

Self-righteousness and presumptive moral judgments pose a great danger in the political arena. To become convinced of the divine infallibility of one's personal predilections on a secular political issue is to play God, to assume to oneself the attributes of deity. It cultivates an arrogant intolerance of dissenting viewpoints and relegates one's political adversaries to the category of evil *per se*.

The New Age (October 1987)

RELIGION IN PUBLIC EDUCATION

241. American Association of School Administrators

If your school district is concerned about appropriate ways to include teaching about religion in your school curriculum, here are some important considerations:

- The study of religions in public schools is permitted by the Constitution as long as the subject matter is presented objectively as part of a secular program of education.
- Teachers of religion courses should be sensitive to varying beliefs of their students.
- The First Amendment does not forbid all mention of religion in the public schools. It does prohibit the advancement or inhibition of religion.
- Public schools are not required to delete from their curriculum materials that may offend any religious sensibility.
- The decision to include—or exclude—material from the curriculum must be based on secular, not religious, reasons.
- The material must be presented objectively.
- Religion should be taught with the same care and discipline as other academic courses.
- Schools should be especially sensitive to the developmental differences between elementary and secondary school students. Subjects or teaching methods that may be appropriate for secondary students may not be appropriate for younger children.

1986

242. Joseph L. Blau

Keeping education in the United States free of sectarian influence has long been one of the primary struggles of believers in freedom of religion.

Cornerstones of Religious Freedom in America (Boston: Beacon Press, 1949)

243. R. Freeman Butts

If the American people wish to adhere to the principle of separation as seen in the long perspective of history, they should decide to prohibit non-sectarian religious instruction in public schools as a form of multiple establishment of religion.

The American Tradition in Religion and Education (Boston: Beacon Press, 1950), p. 189

244. Cincinnati Board of Education

Religious instruction and the reading of religious books, including the Holy Bible, are prohibited in the common schools of Cincinnati. The children of the parents of all sects and opinions, in matters of faith and worship, are to enjoy alike the benefit of the common school fund.

Resolution, 1869

245. Peter W. Cookson Jr.

America needs a vibrant, strong, and democratic public school system because it is the nursery of democracy. Schools can become oases of authenticity in a troubled and often alienating world.

School Choice: The Struggle for the Soul of American Education
(New Haven: Yale University Press, 1994)

246. John Dewey

We are a people of many races, many faiths, creeds, and religions. I do not think that the men who made the Constitution forbade the establishment of a State church because they were opposed to religion. They knew that the introduction of religious differences into American life would undermine the democratic foundations of this country.

What holds for adults holds even more for children, sensitive and conscious of differences. I certainly hope that the Board of Education will think very, very seriously before it introduces this division and antagonism in our public schools.

Testimony at Board of Education hearing, New York City, in opposition to "released time" for religious instruction. *New York Times* (November 14, 1940)

247. Sen. Sam J. Ervin Jr. (D-N.C.)

If religious freedom is to endure in America, the responsibility for teaching religion to public school children must be left to the homes and churches of our land, where this responsibility rightfully belongs. It must not be assumed by the government through the agency of the public school system.

Preserving the Constitution (Charlottesville, Va.: Michie, 1984)

248. *Eugene (Ore.) Register-Guard*

A public school teacher occupies a position of great trust, with potentially great influence over young people whose attendance is compulsory. A person should not be allowed to take advantage of such a position to promote his or her own— or any—religion.

Editorial, January 1984

249. Rabbi Arthur Gilbert

Jews are still disadvantaged in many "Christian countries" where the faithful control the structures of education and impose rites of Christian affirmation on school children as part of school policy. We are concerned . . . when the evangelical purposes of one church or of all churches are supported through disbursements from the public treasury.

Religious Freedom in Jewish Tradition and Experience, 1966

250. Victor Griffin

To preach the gospel of reconciliation while practicing or condoning educational apartheid purely on religious grounds is far removed from the teaching and example of Jesus. In Northern Ireland, religious and political divisions are accentuated and perpetuated by such segregation.

Supplement to his autobiography, *Mark of Protest* (Dublin: Gill & Macmillan, 1993). Griffin was dean of St. Patrick's Cathedral (Anglican) in Dublin, Ireland from 1969 to 1991.

251. *Madison (Wis.) Capital Times*

The simple and lamentable fact is that there is far more prejudice and bigotry about religious matters than most of us want to admit. If sectarian doctrine is introduced into our schools we run the risk of transmitting the prejudices of adults to our children, who, fortunately, are comparatively free of it. The differences which divide adults might well become a part of the life of school children and do serious damage to public education.

Editorial, December 18, 1952

252. Vashti Cromwell McCollum

I simply do not believe it is the function of the public school to bring children into the church or to discipline them if they do not go to church. Public schools should not be recruiting centers for sectarian interests.

One Woman's Fight (New York: Doubleday and Co., Inc., 1951), p. 23

253. Richard C. McMillan

Government sponsored and required acts of religious devotion have no place in a pluralistic society dedicated to religious freedom.

Religion in the Public Schools (Macon, Ga.: Mercer University Press, 1984)

254. *Memphis Commercial Appeal*

Responsibility for religious training rightly rests not with public education but with the family and the religious organization of its choice. Religion in America is strong and free because our founding fathers had the wisdom to separate church and state.

Editorial, July 30, 1980

255. Conrad Henry Moehlman

To call public education godless betrays invincible ignorance, infinite prejudice, and complete misunderstanding of what religion is all about.

School and Church: The American Way (New York: Harper, 1944), pp. 97–98

256. National Education Association

The National Education Association believes that the constitutional provisions on the establishment of and the free exercise of religion in the First Amendment require that there be no sectarian practices in the public school program.

Resolution adopted by Representative Assembly 1978, reaffirmed 1986

257. *New York Times*

It is simply not a legitimate concern of federal educational policy whether the nation's children are being provided adequately with religious values. This is a matter for the home, the churches, and if the parents so desire, the religious schools.

Editorial, August 18, 1971.

258. ———

There can be no religious freedom where any church or group of churches dominates the entire educational system.

Editorial, January 14, 1930

259. Richard V. Pierard

The public schools are one of the few institutions that consciously affirm the tradition of democratic pluralism and constitute a commonality around which all Americans can unite. Certainly they can be improved and the private schools can challenge them to do better, but they are still the one thing that is open to all, regardless of race, creed, sex, or handicap. To give public money to institutions that do not operate on this principle is folly of the first order.

Journal of Church and State 29 (spring 1987): 324

260. Public Education Religion Studies Center (Wright State University)

1. The school may sponsor the study of religion, but may not sponsor the practice of religion.

2. The school may expose students to all religious views, but may not impose any particular view.

3. The school's approach to religion is one of instruction, not one of indoctrination.

4. The function of the school is to educate about all religions, not to convert to any one religion.

5. The school's approach is academic, not devotional.

6. The school should study what all people believe, but should not teach a student what to believe.

7. The school should strive for student awareness of all religions, but should not press for student acceptance of any one religion.

8. The school should seek to inform the student about various beliefs, but should not seek to conform him or her to any one belief.

Guidelines for teaching about religion in public schools, 1981

261. Eleanor Roosevelt

I do not want church groups controlling the schools of our country. They must remain free.

Column, "My Day" (July 8, 1949)

262. ———

Anyone who knows history will recognize that the domination of education or of government by any one particular religious faith is never a happy arrangement for the people.

Letter to Cardinal Spellman, July 23, 1949

263. Benjamin B. Sendor

In the realm of First Amendment case law, court decisions governing the role of religion in public school curriculum exhibit general consistency. This uniformity offers school officials a valuable opportunity to distill coherent, practical lessons from court opinions. The establishment clause permits any instruction—including instruction about the controversial topics of religion, evolution, and sex education—that, by virtue of its form and content, serves secular educational goals. But the establishment clause forbids instruction or the tailoring of instruction with the purpose or primary effect of instilling religious beliefs in children. Although the free exercise clause protects parents and students who oppose such secular instruction, their sole remedy under that clause is partial or total exemption from the courses, not abolition or dilution of the courses.

A Legal Guide to Religion and Public Education, Topeka, Kans., 1988

264. Samuel T. Spear, Episcopal Priest, Brooklyn, N.Y.

The public school, like the state, under whose authority it exists, and by whose taxing power it is supported, should be simply a civil institution, absolutely secular and not at all religious in its purposes, and all practical questions involving this principle should be settled in accordance therewith.

Religion and the State, 1876

265. United Presbyterian Church, U.S.A.

Religious observances . . . and public prayers [in public schools] tend toward indoctrination or meaningless ritual and should be omitted for both reasons.

1964

266. Jesse Ventura, Governor of Minnesota

I believe strongly that government should be encouraging parents to get involved in public schools, instead of giving them vouchers or tax credits so that they can send their kids to private schools. . . . I think we should view our public schools as a good system that's in need of reform, rather than as a broken-down system that we should avoid.

I Ain't Got Time to Bleed (New York: Villard, 1999), p. 20

RELIGIOUS FREEDOM

267. Madeleine Albright, Secretary of State

Religious liberty is an aspiration and an inalienable right of people everywhere. It is central to the strength of free peoples and its protection and promotion are important elements of America's support for human rights around the globe.

A foreword to a State Department report, "United States Policies in Support of Religious Freedom," issued in 1997.

268. ———

Freedom of religion is central to American history and identity . . . and is a fundamental source of our strength in the world.

Ibid.

269. Glenn L. Archer

We must work harder than ever to preserve freedom of religion here in this blessed land. We must not capitulate. Our resolve must not waiver. Much mischief and grief will come from any alliance, holy or otherwise, between organized religious groups and the state.

The Dream Lives On (Washington, D.C.: Robert Luce, 1982), p. 247

270. Baptist World Alliance

We reaffirm our belief in full religious liberty for all persons. This freedom means: to profess openly and confess one's faith even when this involves a change of religious identity; to proclaim one's religious beliefs and experiences; to engage in private and corporate worship; to teach one's religious beliefs and freedom of parents to provide religious instruction and nurture for their children; to advocate greater social justice and social change in the civil order; and freedom for religious groups to conduct their own affairs without outside control or interference and to have property to use for their needs.

We call upon leaders of religious bodies and leaders of national governments to accept, implement, and defend full religious liberty for all persons.

From a resolution adopted by the 13th Congress, Stockholm, July 1975.

271. Thomas F. Bayard, Secretary of State

Religious liberty is the chief cornerstone of the American system of government, and provisions for its security are imbedded in the written charter and interwoven in the moral fabric of its laws.

1885

272. Cardinal Joseph Bernardin

One of the hallmarks of our democratic system of government and our social environment here in the United States is the fact that a plurality of views informs our public discourse regarding fundamental human questions. At times, these views flow from religious beliefs. At other times, they derive from philosophical or pragmatic judgments about the meaning and purpose of life. This pluralism is the result of the free speech accorded by the Constitution to each citizen as well as the right both to freely exercise one's religion and to practice no religion.

Address, University of Chicago Hospital, May 26, 1988

273. Paul Blanshard, Author

Religious liberty in a nation is as real as the liberty of its least popular religious minority. Look not to the size of cathedrals or even to the words on the statute books for proof of the reality of religious freedom. Ask what is the fate of the Protestant in Spain, the Jew in Saudi Arabia, the Arab in Israel, the Catholic in Poland or the atheist in the United States.

Address, Orlando, Fla., February 1974

274. Joseph L. Blau

Freedom of religion means the right of the individual to choose and to adhere to whichever religious beliefs he may prefer, to join with others in religious associations to express these beliefs, and to incur no civil disabilities because of his choice.

Cornerstones of Religious Freedom in America (Boston: Beacon Press, 1949)

275. ———

Those who accept freedom of religion as a right are obligated by this acceptance to take the maintenance of freedom of religion as a duty.

Ibid.

276. ———

Since 1787 the principle of freedom of religion has been attacked but never overthrown.

Ibid.

277. Rep. Sherwood Boehlert (R-N.Y.)

The United States remains a beacon and a sanctuary for those seeking religious freedom.

Address, U.S. House of Representatives, June 4, 1998

278. Morton Borden

One must keep in mind that religious liberty did not come easily. It did not simply ripen and fall to nonChristians as a gift. It had to be fought for in the legislative halls, in constitutional conventions and in the courts. What has been achieved, easily can be lost.

Reason magazine (June 1987)

279. President James Buchanan

[The Government of the United States] possesses no power whatever over the question of religion. All denominations of Christians stand on the same footing in this country—and every man enjoys the inestimable right of worshipping his God according to the dictates of his own conscience.

Leo F. Stock, *U.S. Ministers to the Papal States* (Washington, D.C.: Catholic University Press, 1933), p. 213

280. Charles Carroll

I do hereby recommend to the present and future generations the principles of that important document as the best earthly inheritance their ancestors could bequeath to them, and pray that the civil and religious liberties they have secured to my country may be perpetuated to the remotest posterity and extended to the whole family of man.

Kate M. Rowland, *The Life and Correspondence of Charles Carroll of Carrollton, 1737–1832,*
vol. 2 (New York: 1898), title page. Carroll was the only Catholic to sign the Declaration of Independence.
As the only surviving signer, Carroll wrote these words on July 4, 1826, on a copy of the
Declaration of Independence that is preserved in the New York Public Library.

281. The Charter of Liberties and Privileges

No person or persons which profess faith in God by Jesus Christ, shall at any time be anyway molested, punished, disquieted, or called in question for any difference in opinion or matter of religious concernment . . . but all and every such person or persons may from time to time and at all times freely have and freely enjoy his or their judgments or consciences in matters of religion throughout all the Provinces. . . .

Promulgated by Thomas Dongan, governor of New York, and his popular assembly,
meeting at Fort James, October 14, 1683. Dongan was a Roman Catholic. See Thomas P. Phelan,
Thomas Dongan, Colonial Governor of New York, 1683–1688 (New York: P. J. Kenedy, 1933), p. 43.

282. Sanford H. Cobb

Here, among all the benefits to mankind to which this soil has given rise, this pure religious liberty may be justly rated as the great gift of America to civilization and the world.

The Rise of Religious Liberty in America (New York: The Macmillan Company, 1902), p. 2

283. Henry Steele Commager

The Americans who framed our Constitution felt that without freedom of religion no other freedom counted.

"The Right to Believe," ABC-TV documentary, March 30, 1975

284. ———

[T]he decision for complete religious freedom and for separation of church and state in the eyes of the rest of the world [was] perhaps the most important decision reached in the New World. Everywhere in the western world of the eighteenth century, church and state were one; and everywhere the state maintained an established church and tried to force conformity to its dogma.

The British had attempted—half-heartedly—to extend the Anglican Establishment to America, but they had, on the whole, permitted a good deal of religious freedom and independence. When the American states became independent they inevitably threw off the Anglican Establishment. A few of them tried to keep an establishment of their own, but given the pluralism of American religion, that attempt was clearly foredoomed.

Virginia led the way by announcing not only complete religious freedom, but the separation of church and state, and thereafter, one after another, all the original states followed this principle. When James Madison introduced the Bill of Rights to the first Congress, the very first of them embraced freedom of religion, and that was adopted by the Congress and by the states, and incorporated as a fundamental article of American constitutionalism.

Thus the new United States took the lead among the nations of the earth in the establishment of religious freedom. That is one reason America has never had any religious wars or any religious persecutions.

Modern Maturity (June–July 1976)

285. *Commonweal*

The First Amendment prohibiting the establishment of religion and guaranteeing freedom of religion, speech, press, and political activity, is not to be tampered with.

Editorial, December 8, 1978

286. Norman Cousins

Freedom of religion, as the Founding Fathers saw it, was not just the right to associate oneself with a certain denomination but the right to disassociate, without penalty. Belief or nonbelief was a matter of individual choice—a right underwritten in the basic charter of the nation's liberties.

Saturday Review (December 1980)

287. ———

In the relationship of government to religion, there was a solid ring of conviction that tied the Founding Fathers to each other. The government was not to take upon itself the responsibility to determine the religion of its people. . . . This necessarily meant that guarantees of religious freedom must apply to believers and nonbelievers alike. The right of an individual to worship in his own way or not to worship at all was part of the protection of a free society.

In God We Trust: The Religious Beliefs and Ideas of the American Founding Fathers
(New York: Harper & Brothers Publishers, 1958), p. 13

288. Rev. Charles E. Curran

In general Roman Catholic and mainline Protestant Christianity contributed little or nothing to the original acceptance of religious liberty in the West. Church and theological support for religious liberty in the West came only after religious liberty had been well accepted in the world at large.

"Religious Freedom—Human Rights in the World and the Church" in Religious Liberty and Human Rights, edited by Leonard Swidler (Philadelphia: Ecumenical Press, 1986), p. 145

289. Cardinal Richard Cushing, Archbishop of Boston

The church must show herself as a champion of religious liberty.

Address, St. Peter's Basilica, September 23, 1964

290. Edd Doerr, Executive Director, Americans for Religious Liberty

Religious freedom, to many Fourth of July orators, is simply a matter of one's being free to believe as one pleases and to attend the church or synagogue of one's choice. This definition *will not do*, neither here and now, nor in any place at any time.

Religious freedom, real religious freedom—as that concept has been forged into shape over the centuries on the anvil of practical experience by Madisons and Jeffersons, by far-sighted judges and lawmakers and religious leaders, by writers and ordinary people—means at least this:

It means the right to worship or not to worship, to be or not to be a member of a religious group, to change or discontinue a religious affiliation. It means the right to express one's religious views and to attempt to persuade others of their correctness, the right to travel for religious purposes, the right to use one's home and property for religious purposes.

Religious freedom means the right to live one's life according to one's own beliefs, up to the point, of course, at which that free exercise of religion begins to interfere with the equal rights of another person. It means the right to make and follow one's own moral judgments and decisions of conscience on such matters as marriage and reproduction. It means the right to provide religious and moral instruction to one's children. It includes the right to access to information and opinion.

Religious freedom means the right to determine whether and to what extent one will contribute to the support of any or all religious institutions or programs. It means no taxation whatsoever for any religious institutions or programs, as Madison made clear 205 years ago in his Memorial and Remonstrance Against Religious Assessments, in which he declared that such "establishments of religion" inevitably produce "bigotry and persecution."

As religious freedom includes the right of persons to form or belong to religious or lifestance organizations, these associations must enjoy the freedom to order their own worship, educational, charitable, and other activities; to formulate and change their teachings and doctrines; to determine their own forms of organization and governance; to set their own standards for membership and positions of authority; to operate programs of missionary outreach; to interpret to the public their views and principles.

Religious liberty means that government may not discriminate against or in favor of any person because of his or her religious beliefs or disbeliefs, for religious association membership or nonmembership. It means that government may not impose religious tests for public office or enact policies based on principles that depend for their validity on the doctrines or ethos of particular religious bodies.

Full religious freedom requires, as Jefferson insisted in 1802, referring to the First Amendment, that there be a "wall of separation between church and state."

The edifice of religious freedom, though still not completed, is one of the grandest and most magnificent ever erected by humankind. Yet it rests on the not always steady shoulders of all of us, of We the People. We must never allow it to wobble, to crack, to erode, or to be destroyed. We must resolve that that shall not happen.

> Address, Touro Synagogue, Newport, RI, August 19, 1990, at a celebration of
> George Washington's August 1790 letter to the Jewish Community of Newport.

291. Justice William O. Douglas

The religious freedom which the First Amendment protects has many facets:

1. No sectarian authority shares in the power of government nor sits in its councils.

2. Government has no directive influence in any of the affairs of any church.

3. Citizens are not taxed for the support of any religious institution and no church has any claim on any of the public revenues.

4. People can belong to any church they desire—or to none at all; and no one is bound to have a ceremony such as marriage performed by any sectarian authority.

5. In disputes between sects or factions of a church over the management of church affairs the civil courts apply not the law applicable to secular affairs but the law that the governing bodies of the church have provided to govern their internal affairs.

6. Public schools are not proper agencies for religious education, though there is no constitutional reason why the state cannot adjust the schedules of the public schools to allow time for the students to get religious instruction elsewhere.

7. Parents and children have the privilege of patronizing private religious schools, rather than public ones, if they so desire.

8. An exercise or ritual may not be exacted by the state from an individual, if it runs counter to his religious convictions.

9. Religious liberty includes not only the conventional methods of worship but the unorthodox as well, such as distributing religious literature from door to door.

10. No license may be exacted by the state for the performance of any religious exercise nor a tax imposed on it.

11. Although the matter has not been authoritatively decided, it would seem that religious liberty extends to atheists as well as to theists, to those who find their religion in ethics and morality, rather than in a Supreme Being.

12. What may be pagan exercises to one person may be a devotional to another. In general it is no business of the government what rite or practice a person selects as a part of his religious beliefs; and he may not be punished for practicing or avowing it.

The Right of the People (New York: Doubleday, 1958), pp. 91–92

292. Edict of Milan

It accords with the good order of the realm and the peacefulness of our times that each should have freedom to worship God after his own choice; and we do not intend to detract from the honor due to any religion or its followers.

Proclaimed by Emperors Constantine and Licinius, 313 C.E.

293. Edward L. Ericson,
Cofounder of Americans for Religious Liberty

The historic alliance of liberal and evangelical forces, joined in support of freedom of thought and the separation of church and state, brought into being and sustains our pluralistic secular democracy. The secular democratic state is the surest protector of religious and intellectual liberty ever crafted by human ingenuity. Nothing is more fallacious, or inimical to genuine religious liberty, than the seductive notion that the state should "favor" or "foster" religion. All history testifies that such practices inevitably result in favoring one religion over less powerful minorities and secular opinion.

In the long run governmental favoritism vitiates the religious spirit itself. Where in the Western world is organized religion stronger than in the United States where the church is a take-your-choice affair? Where is it weaker than in Europe where sophisticated secularists joke that they have been "inoculated" for life against religion by compulsory religious indoctrination in state schools? Preserving the secular character of government and the public school is the surest guarantee that religion in America will remain free, vital, uncorrupted by political power, and independent of state manipulation.

American Freedom and the Radical Right (New York: Frederick Ungar, 1982)

294. Sen. Sam J. Ervin Jr. (D-N.C.)

Religious liberty is the great contribution this nation has made to the world in both the realm of politics and religion.

Address, Nashville, Tenn., February 22, 1966

295. ———

What James Madison and the other men of his generation had in mind when they wrote the First Amendment was that there should be no official relationship of any character between government and any church or many churches, and no levying of taxes for the support of any church, or many churches, or all churches, or any institution conducted by any of them.

Address, U.S. Senate, April 23, 1973

296. ———

I believe in a wall between church and state so high that no one can climb over it.

When religion controls government, political liberty dies; and when government controls religion, religious liberty perishes.

Every American has the constitutional right not to be taxed or have his tax money expended for the establishment of religion.

For too long the issue of government aid to church related organizations has been a divisive force in our society and in the Congress. It has erected communication barriers among our religions and fostered intolerance.

Quotations from Chairman Sam: The Wit and Wisdom of Senator Sam Ervin
(New York: Harper & Row, 1973)

297. ———

Government is contemptuous of true religion when it confiscates the taxes of Caesar to finance the things of God.

"Open Letter to President Reagan," *Congressional Record*, April 29, 1982

298. ———

A school prayer amendment would confer upon public school boards a power the First Amendment now denies to Congress and the states, that is, the power to establish religion.

Preserving the Constitution (Charlottesville, Va.: Michie, 1984)

299. ———

If religious freedom is to endure in America, the responsibility for teaching religion to public school children must be left to the homes and churches of our land, where this responsibility rightfully belongs. It must not be assumed by the government through the agency of the public school system.

Ibid.

300. ———

Religious freedom is America's most precious possession and must be preserved irrespective of its cost.

American Legion Magazine, March 1985

301. The Flushing Remonstrance

We welcome any sons of Adam who come in love among us and will not condemn, punish, banish, prosecute or lay violent hands upon anyone, in whatever name, form or title he might appear. We are true subjects of both the church and the state and we are bound by the law of God and man to do good unto all men, and evil to no man.

This document was drawn up and signed by 31 townsmen of the village of Flushing, New Netherland (New York), in 1657, to protest the persecution of Quakers by colonial governor Peter Stuyvesant. A U.S. postage stamp was issued in 1957 to commemorate the tricentennial of this event.

302. Marvin E. Frankel, U.S. District Judge

Fortunately, despite the appearance of petty inquisitors from time to time, the pressure for orthodoxy in religious conceptions has never prevailed in America. There can be no heresy here. Or blasphemy. We are all free to believe as we please. And none of us is entitled to force beliefs on others. Above all, no person and no church is brigaded with the power of the state or condemned to be coerced by the state in matters of conscience. An inheritance that includes these principles is priceless. We owe ourselves and our posterity the duty to preserve it.

Faith and Freedom: Religious Liberty in America (New York: Hill and Wang, 1994), p. 18

303. Robert T. Handy, Professor of Church History

The passage of the First Amendment is the single most dramatic and significant turning point of a revolutionary transition to religious freedom.

"Religious Freedom's Magna Charta" in *Union Seminary Quarterly Review* 38 (1984): 303

304. ———

Inasmuch as we Americans have grown up under the conditions of religious freedom, we often too easily forget that it came about only after centuries of

struggle. Freedom in matters of religion was bought at a price—and for some
courageous persons in the past, the cost was high.

Foreword to Glenn T. Miller, *Religious Liberty in America* (Philadelphia: Westminster Press, 1976), p. 11

305. Archbishop John Ireland

Religious freedom is the basic life of America, the cement running through all
its walls and battlements, the safeguard of its peace and prosperity.

Essays in the American Catholic Tradition, edited by P. Albert Duhamed
(New York: Rinehart & Company, Inc., 1960), p. 139

306. President Thomas Jefferson

The Virginia Act for religious freedom has been received with infinite approbation in Europe and propagated with enthusiasm. . . . It is honorable for us to
have produced the first legislature who had the courage to declare that the
reason of man may be trusted with the formation of his own opinions.

Quoted in Dumas Malone, *Jefferson the Virginian* (Boston: Little, Brown, 1948), p. 279

307. ———

[W]e have solved by fair experiment the great and interesting question whether freedom of religion is compatible with order in government and obedience to the laws.

Letter to James Madison, December 16, 1786

308. ———

In reviewing the history of the times through which we have passed, no portion of
it gives greater satisfaction or reflection, than that which represents the efforts of
the friends of religious freedom and the success with which they are crowned.

Henry Wilder Foote, *Thomas Jefferson: Champion of Religious Freedom* (Boston: Beacon Press, 1947)

309. ———

I am for freedom of religion and against all maneuvers to bring about a legal
ascendancy of one sect over another.

Letter to Elbridge Gerry, January 26, 1799

310. ———

I am really mortified to be told that, *in the United States of America*, a fact like this can become a subject to inquiry, and of criminal inquiry too, as an offence against religion; that a question about the sale of a book can be carried before the civil magistrate. Is this then our freedom of religion?

Letter to N. G. Dufief, April 19, 1814, referring to the legal problems attending issuance of a scientific work by French author M. de Becourt on the creation of the world.

311. Pope John XXIII

Also among man's rights is the right to be able to worship God in accordance with the right dictates of his own conscience, and to profess his religion both in private and in public.

Encyclical, *Pacem in Terris*, 1963

312. Adrienne Koch, Historian

Religious liberty Madison found to be the first component of human freedom, for if the mind and conscience are captive, the man is. Civil liberties presuppose religious liberty for Madison, and what a shorthand language calls the affairs of church and state stands for a wider context of respect for the inquiring, the creative creature.

Madison's *"Advice to My Country"* (Princeton, N.J.: Princeton University Press, 1966), p. xvii

313. Abbé Hugues-Felicité Robert de Lamennais

Each day one understands more and more that political liberty is bound insep-arably to religious liberty. It has its roots in it and cannot be affirmed and devel-oped other than through it.

L'Avenir (August 1831), a progressive French Catholic journal of opinion edited by Abbé Lamennais

314. President James Madison

Freedom arises from a multiplicity of sects, which pervades America, and which is the best and only security for religious liberty in any society.

Address to Virginia Constitutional Convention, June 12, 1788

315. William Martin

America, though not perfect in its record of religious tolerance, has been remarkable in its success at avoiding wars over differing faiths and, overall, at granting freedom to a wide variety of religious expressions and practices. That is a notable achievement in human history, and one of our nation's most admirable accomplishments.

With God on Our Side: The Rise of the Religious Right in America
(New York: Broadway Books, 1997), p. 371

316. Maryland Toleration Act

Noe person or persons whatsoever within this Province, or the Islands, Ports, Harbors, Creekes, or havens thereunto belonging professing to believe in Jesus Christ, shall from henceforth bee any waies troubled, Molested or discountenanced for or in respect of his or her religion or in the free exercise thereof within this Province or the Islands thereunto belonging nor any way compelled to the beliefe of any other Religion against his or her consent.

April 21, 1649

317. George Mason

That religion, or the duty which we owe to our Creator, and the manner of discharging it, can be directed only by reason and conviction, not by force or violence; and therefore all men are equally entitled to the free exercise of religion, according to the dictates of conscience; and that it is the mutual duty of all to practice Christian forebearance, love, and charity towards each other.

Virginia Bill of Rights, 1776

318. Massachusetts Bill of Rights

It is the right as well as the duty of all men in society, publicly, and at stated seasons, to worship the Supreme Being, the Great Creator, and Preserver of the universe. And no subject shall be hurt, molested, or restrained, in his person, liberty, or estate, for worshipping God in the manner and season most agreeable to the dictates of his own conscience.

1780

319. Giovanni Miegge

Religious liberty is primarily a man's liberty to profess a faith different from that of the dominant religion, and to unite in public worship with those who share his faith.

Religious Liberty (New York: Association Press, 1957)

320. Montalembert, Nineteenth-Century French Catholic Liberal

Religious liberty, sincere and equal for all, without privilege . . . in a word the free church in a free nation, such has been the program which inspired my first efforts and which I have persevered, after thirty years of struggle, in considering just and reasonable.

Quoted in M. Searle Bates, *Religious Liberty: An Inquiry*
(New York: International Missionary Council, 1945), p. 196

321. Rev. John Courtney Murray

The right to religious freedom has its foundation, not in the church or society or the state, but in the very dignity of the human person.

We Hold These Truths (New York: Sheed & Ward, 1960)

322. William Penn

Is it not true that persecution against persons exercising their liberty of conscience reduces the honor of God? Does it not also defile the Christian religion, violate the authority of Scripture, and go against the principles of common reason? Finally, does it not destroy the well-being of government itself?

Concerning the honor of God, we say that restraint and persecution for matters relating to conscience directly invade the divine right, and rob the Almighty of that which belongs to none but Himself. . . .

The Great Case of Liberty of Conscience (London, 1670), p. 1

323. *The Rakovian Catechism*

Let everyone be free to express his judgment in religious matters. . . . In so far as we are concerned, we are all brothers, and no power, no authority has been given us over the consciences of others.

Preface to the 1665 edition of a 1605 Unitarian confession of faith,
written in Polish by Faustus Socinus

324. Norman Redlich

When the founders put the religious clauses first in the first amendment, it was because of a clear recognition that freedom of religion was essential to political democracy.

Testimony for the American Jewish Congress, U.S. Senate Hearings,
Committee on the Judiciary, September 16, 1982

325. President Franklin D. Roosevelt

Embodied in the federal Constitution and ingrained in our hearts and souls is the national conviction that every man has an inalienable right to worship God according to the dictates of his own conscience.

Quoted in Frank Kingdon, ed., *As FDR Said: A Treasury of His Speeches, Conversations and Writings*
(New York: Duell, Sloan and Pearce, 1950), p. 153

326. President Theodore Roosevelt

If there is one thing for which we stand in this country, it is for complete religious freedom, and it is an emphatic negation of this right to cross-examine a man on his religion before being willing to support him for office.

Letter to J. C. Martin, November 9, 1908

327. Clinton Rossiter, Historian

The establishment of religious freedom was no less momentous an achievement than the clearing of the great forest or the winning of independence, for the twin doctrines of separation of church and state and liberty of individual conscience are the marrow of our democracy, if not indeed America's most magnificent contribution to the freeing of Western man.

The American Quest (New York: Harcourt, Brace, 1971)

328. Philip Schaff, Historian

The relationship of church and state in the United States secures full liberty of religious thought, speech, and action, within the limits of the public peace and order. It makes persecution impossible.

Religion and liberty are inseparable. Religion is voluntary, and cannot, and ought not to be forced. This is a fundamental article of the American creed, without distinction of sect or party. Liberty, both civil and religious, is an American instinct.

Such liberty is impossible on the basis of a union of church and state, where the one of necessity restricts or controls the other. It requires a friendly separation, where each power is entirely independent in its own sphere.

Church and State in the United States (G. P. Putnam's Sons, 1888), pp. 9–10

329. Second Vatican Council

This Vatican Council declares that the human person has a right to religious freedom. This freedom means that all men are to be immune from coercion on the part of individuals or of social groups and of any human power, in such ways that no one is to be forced to act in a manner contrary to his own beliefs. . . .

The Council further declares that the right to religoius freedom has its foundation in the very dignity of the human person, as this dignity is known through the revealed Word of God and by reason itself. This right of the human person to religious liberty is to be recognized in the constitutional law whereby society is governed, and thus it is to become a civil right.

Declaration on Religious Freedom, approved December 7, 1965,
by the world's Roman Catholic Bishops by a vote of 2,308 to 70.
Reprinted in Louis Janssens, *Freedom of Conscience and Religious Freedom*
(Staten Island, N.Y.: Alba House, 1965), pp. 146–47.

330. Paul D. Simmons

Religious liberty does not mean the freedom of a religious sect or a combination of groups to organize for a political takeover and impose religious beliefs or requirements upon minorities.

Freedom of Conscience (Amherst, N.Y.: Prometheus Books, 2000), p. 55

331. Alfred E. Smith, Governor of New York, Democratic Candidate for President, 1928

I believe in absolute freedom of conscience for all men and equality of all churches, all sects and all beliefs before the law as a matter of right and not as a matter of favor. I believe in the absolute separation of church and state and in the strict enforcement of the Constitution that Congress shall make no law respecting an establishment of religion or prohibiting the free exercise thereof. I believe that no tribunal of any church has any power to make any decree of any force in the law of the land, other than to establish the status of its own communicants within its own church.

Atlantic Monthly (April 1927)

332. Statement by Four Religious Leaders

Religious freedom, based on the separation principle, has been the keystone of all our other freedoms. Freedom of religion has made possible our pluralistic society, with its capacity for negotiating and reconciling religious conflicts and differences that have so often plunged other societies into strife, misery, and bloodshed.

To create religious voting blocs on the American scene would be to discard these historic achievements—to invite a return to religious strife or oppression. It could bring us back to the conditions of colonial times, when theocratic rulers withheld religious liberty from the people.

Issued by Episcopal Bishop Paul Moore, Dr. Arnold Olson of the Evangelical Free Church, Rabbi Marc H. Tanenbaum of the American Jewish Committee, and Rev. Joseph O'Hare, editor of *America*, on October 18, 1976.

333. Justice Joseph Story

If there is any right sacred beyond all others, because it imports everlasting consequences, it is the right to worship God according to the dictates of our own consciences.

Joseph L. Blau, *Cornerstones of Religious Freedom in America* (Boston: Beacon Press, 1949), p. 125

334. Tertullian

It is a fundamental human right, a privilege of nature, that every man should worship according to his own convictions.

Ad Scapulam, 202 C.E.

335. Benjamin F. Underwood

Thankful for all the blessings that have been secured to us by the struggles and sacrifices of our fathers, let us show our gratitude and pay the debt we owe them to those who shall come after us, by adding to what we have received in strengthening the foundations of freedom, so that no fury of religious fanaticism will ever be able to destroy them. Long live the Republic! May she continue to grow in greatness and grandeur till her light and glory shall fill the earth.

Joseph L. Blau, *Cornerstones of Religious Freedom in America* (Boston: Beacon Press, 1949)

336. United Methodist Church

In the modern world, every person—individually or in association with others —should be free to hold or change religious beliefs; to express religious beliefs in worship, teaching and practice; and to proclaim and act upon the implications of religious beliefs for relationships in a social and political community.

We support the explicit constitutional safeguards which have long undergirded religious liberty in the United States of America. We believe it is of utmost importance for all persons, religious groups, and governments to maintain a continuing vigilance to insure that religious liberty be guaranteed. We respectfully request all national churches within the fellowship of the world United Methodist family to continue to work for the realization and support of religious liberty in the constitutions, governmental forms, and social practices of their respective countries.

Religious freedom is of three kinds. (1) The freedom to worship and believe with integrity—that is, without being required by any external authority to affirm beliefs that one does not hold or to engage in acts of worship that do not conform to one's inner state of mind. This form of freedom must be considered absolute. (2) The freedom to communicate the meaning of one's religious convictions to others. This freedom should be considered a near absolute, subject only to the limitation that verbal injury to others and direct incitement to criminal actions cannot be permitted legal refuge on grounds of religious motivation. (3) The

freedom to act on the basis of one's religious convictions. This freedom may sometimes be limited in the regulation of human affairs, for the sake of public health
and safety, or to guarantee the rights of others. Nevertheless, the widest possible
latitude should also be provided for the expression of this form of religious liberty.

. . . The constitutional provisions which preclude governments from taking
any action "respecting an establishment of religion" has a positive effect on the
maintenance of religious liberty. "Establishment of religion" places the power of
all society behind the religious expressions of some part of society. The United
Methodist Church is opposed to all establishment of religion by government.
Therefore, we are in agreement with the Supreme Court's decisions declaring
unconstitutional required worship services as part of the public school program.
We believe these decisions enhance and strengthen religious liberty within the
pluralism that characterizes the United States of America.

. . . We recognize that religious liberty includes the freedom of an individual
to be agnostic, a non-theist, an atheist, or even an anti-theist. Otherwise, the
civil community would be invested with authority to establish orthodoxy in matters of belief. We are confident that such a state of affairs would constitute a
threat to all religious interests. According to the ethical concept of a responsible
society, government commits a morally indefensible act when it imposes upon
its people—by force, fear, or other means—the profession or refutation of any
belief. Theologically speaking, religious liberty is the freedom that God has
given, in his creative act, to all persons to think and to choose belief in God for
themselves, including the freedom to doubt and deny God.

We recognize that civil authorities have often been leaders in expanding
religious liberty. Many times in history it has been constitutions, legislatures,
and courts that have served as protectors of religious liberty against the misuse
of governmental powers by religious bodies.

. . . We believe in the principle of universal public education, and we reaffirm our support of public educational institutions. At the same time, we recognize and pledge our continued allegiance to the U.S. Constitutional principle
that citizens have a right to establish and maintain private schools from private
resources so long as such schools meet public standards of quality. Such schools
have made a genuine contribution to society. We do not support the expansion
or the strengthening of private schools with public funds. Furthermore, we
oppose the establishment or strengthening of private schools that jeopardize the
public school system or thwart valid public policy.

We specifically oppose tuition tax credits or any other mechanism which directly or indirectly allows government funds to support religious schools at the primary and secondary level. Persons of one particular faith should be free to use their own funds to strengthen the belief system of their particular religious group. But they should not expect all taxpayers, including those who adhere to other religious belief systems, to provide funds to teach religious views with which they do not agree. . . .

We live in a pluralistic society. In such a society, churches should not seek to use the authority of government to make the whole community conform to their particular moral codes. Rather, churches should seek to enlarge and clarify the ethical grounds of public discourse and to identify and define the foreseeable consequences of available choices of public policy.

In participating in the arena of public affairs, churches are not inherently superior to other participants; hence the stands which they take on particular issues of public policy are not above question or criticism. . . .

Finally, churches should not seek to utilize the processes of public affairs to further their own institutional interests or to obtain special privileges for themselves.

Excerpts from General Assembly Resolution, 1980

337. United Nations

Everyone has the right to freedom of thought, conscience and religion; this right includes freedom to change his religion or belief, either alone or in community with others and in public or private, to manifest his religion or belief in teaching, practice, worship, and observance.

Article 18, United Nations Universal Declaration of Human Rights, 1948

338. ———

Everyone shall have the right to freedom of thought, conscience, and religion. This right shall include freedom to have a religion or whatever belief of his choice and freedom, either individually or in community with others and in public or private, to manifest his religion or belief in worship, observance, practice, and teaching.

Declaration on the Elimination of All Forms of Intolerance and of Discrimination Based on Religion or Belief, Approved by the General Assembly, November 25, 1981.

339. Queen Victoria, 1858

Firmly relying ourselves on the truth of Christianity and acknowledging with gratitude the solace of religion, we disclaim alike the right and desire to impose our convictions on any of our subjects, but declare it to be our royal will and pleasure that none be in any wise favored, or molested or disquieted by reason of their religious faith or observances, but that all shall alike enjoy the equal and impartial protection of the law; and we do strictly charge and enjoin all those who may be in authority under us that they abstain from all interference with religious belief or worship of any of our subjects on pain of our highest displeasure.

Quoted in Ninan Koshy, *Religious Freedom in a Changing World*
(Geneva: WCC Publications, 1992), p. 33.

340. President George Washington

Every man, conducting himself as a good citizen, and being accountable to God alone for his religious opinions, ought to be protected in worshipping the Deity according to the dictates of his own conscience.

Letter to the United Baptist Chamber of Virginia, May 1789

341. ———

If I could have entertained the slightest apprehension, that the constitution framed in the convention, where I had the honor to preside, might possibly endanger the religious rights of any ecclesiastical society, certainly I would never have placed my signature to it. . . .

If I could conceive that the general government might ever be so administered as to render the liberty of conscience insecure, I beg you will be persuaded, that no one would be more zealous than myself to establish effectual barriers against the horrors of spiritual tyranny, and every species of religious persecution.

Ibid.

342. ———

It is now no more that toleration is spoken of as if it was by the indulgence of one class of the people that another enjoyed the exercise of their inherent natural rights. For happily the Government of the United States, which gives to bigotry no sanction, to persecution no assistance, requires only that those who live under its protection should demean themselves as good citizens in giving it, on all occasions, their effectual support.

Letter to the congregation of Touro Synagogue, Newport, R.I., August 1790

343. ———

Of all the animosities which have existed among mankind, those which are caused by a difference of sentiments in religion appear to be the most inveterate and distressing, and ought to be deprecated.

Letter to Edward Newenham, October 20, 1792

344. ———

We have abundant reason to rejoice that in this Land the light of truth and reason has triumphed over the power of bigotry and superstition, and that every person may here worship God according to the dictates of his own heart. In this enlightened Age and in this Land of equal liberty it is our boast, that a man's religious tenets will not forfeit the protection of the Laws, nor deprive him of the right of attaining and holding the highest offices that are known in the United States.

Letter to the members of the New Church in Baltimore, January 27, 1793

345. ———

The liberty enjoyed by the People of these States of worshipping Almighty God agreeable to their consciences is not only among the choicest of their blessings but also of their rights.

Letter to the Religious Society called the Quakers, September 28, 1789

346. ———

Government being, among other purposes, instituted to protect the consciences of men from oppression, it certainly is the duty of rulers, not only to abstain from it themselves, but according to their stations, to prevent it in others.

Ibid.

Note: The above letters of George Washington are included in Paul F. Boller Jr., *George Washington and Religion* (Dallas: Southern Methodist University Press, 1963).

347. Rufus V. Weaver

Everywhere all who cherish religious liberty should break through every hindering barrier to unite in the support of this common cause.

Champions of Religious Liberty (Nashville: Broadman, 1947), p. 12

348. Samuel West

For the civil authority to pretend to establish particular modes of faith and forms of worship, and to punish all that deviate from the standards which our superiors have set up, is attended with the most pernicious consequences to society. It cramps all free and rational inquiry, fills the world with hypocrites and superstitious bigots—nay, with infidels and skeptics; it exposes men of religion and conscience to the rage and malice of fiery, blind zealots, and dissolves every tender tie of human nature. And I cannot but look upon it as a peculiar blessing of Heaven that we live in a land where everyone can freely deliver his sentiments upon religious subjects, and have the privilege of worshipping God according to the dictates of his own conscience, without any molestation or disturbance—a privilege which I hope we shall ever keep up and strenuously maintain.

Dartmouth, Mass., Election Sermon, 1776

349. Roger Williams

Enforced uniformity confounds civil and religious liberty and denies the principles of Christianity and civility.

That cannot be a true religion which needs carnal weapons to uphold it.

No man shall be required to worship or maintain a worship against his will.

The Bloody Tenet of Persecution (1640)

350. James E. Wood Jr., Director of J. M. Dawson Institute of Church-State Studies, Baylor University

Today religious liberty has become an international necessity. The international dimension of contemporary life inevitably requires all world faiths to espouse religious liberty for all men everywhere since an international community could not prosper without some minimum assurances of tolerance and religious liberty. Special privileges have become a practical impossibility. The growing interrelatedness among all nations has underscored in the modern world that if peace and harmony are to be established and maintained among mankind, it is essential that guarantees of religious liberty be constitutionally provided everywhere. Hence, religious liberty has become a practical necessity.

Church & State (February 1977)

351. Carl Zollman

There is no country in which not only religious liberty in general, but the property of religious bodies in particular, is as secure as it is in the United States.

American Church Law (Egan, Minn.: West, 1933), p. 10

352. ———

Every individual has by nature the inherent, inalienable, and indefeasible right of worshipping and serving God in the mode most consistent with the dictates of his conscience; that none shall be deprived of this right; that no human authority shall in any case interfere with or in any manner control or infringe it; and that the free exercise and enjoyment of religious faith, worship, belief, sentiment, and profession shall forever be allowed, secured, protected, guaranteed, and held sacred. It follows that every person is at liberty to profess and by argument to maintain his opinion in matters of religion; that every denomination is to be equally protected by suitable laws in the peaceable enjoyment of its own mode of public worship; that none will be subordinated to any other or receive any peculiar privileges or advantages—in short, that no preference will be given to nor discrimination made against any religious establishment, church, sect, creed, society or denomination or any form of religious faith or worship or system of ecclesiastical policy. Absolute freedom to choose such religious belief as his judgment and conscience may approve has thus become the birthright of American citizenship. Any civil or political rights, privileges, capacities, or positions which a person may have or hold will not be diminished or enlarged or in any other manner affected by his religious faith, nor will he be disqualified from the performance of his public or private duties on account thereof. He will not, on account of his religious opinion, persuasion, profession, and sentiments or the peculiar mode or manner of his religious worship, be hurt, molested, disturbed, restrained, burdened, or made to suffer in his person or property.

Ibid., pp. 18–19. This is a classic definition of religious liberty as it has developed in the American experience.

RELIGIOUS NEUTRALITY

353. Edwin S. Gaustad

What good deed can government do for religion? The best deed of all: leave it free and unencumbered, burdened by neither enmity nor amity.

Faith of Our Fathers (New York: Harper and Row 1987), p. 137

354. John Leland

Government has no more to do with the religious opinions of men than it has with the principles of mathematics.

Rights of Conscience and Therefore Religious Opinions Not Cognizable by Law (1791)

355. Norman Redlich

If the establishment clause was based on any values at all in our history, it was based on the value of neutrality, it was based on the value of no prescribed religious faith, and it was based on the value of no coercion.

Testimony for the American Jewish Congress, U.S. Senate Hearings, Committee on the Judiciary, September 16, 1982

RELIGIOUS PERSECUTION

356. Hazrat Mirza Tahir Ahmad

People who persecute in the name of religion are totally ignorant of the essence of religion.

Murder in the Name of Allah (London: Lutterworth Press, 1989)

357. The American Baptist Bill of Rights

Believing religious liberty to be not only an inalienable human right, but indispensable to human welfare . . . baptists condemn every form of compulsion in religion or restraint of the free consideration of the claims of religion.

The Road to Freedom of Religion, Rufus W. Weaver, ed. (1944), pp. 17–18.
This statement was approved by four U.S. Baptist denominations.

358. Athanasius, Bishop of Alexandria

It is not by the sword or the spear, by soldiers or by armed force that truth is to be promoted, but by counsel and gentle persuasion.

Quoted in M. Searle Bates, *Religious Liberty: An Inquiry* (New York: International Missionary Council, 1945).

359. Bert B. Beach, Seventh-day Adventist Religious Liberty Executive

There is little doubt that religious liberty is best exercised within the setting of the secular state. This does not mean the state should be hostile or indifferent to religious bodies, but rather that it must exhibit what has been called a "benevolent neutrality." . . .

Freedom of religion also implies the right not to have or profess a religion. This is sometimes overlooked. It is a sad commentary on religion that religionists, probably quite well-meaning at times, have throughout history tried to force fellow human beings into a required religious mold. Apart from the very wrong theological assumptions involved, this is a flagrant violation of the dignity of the human person. Coerced religion is demeaning and of little value.

Bright Candle of Courage (Pacific Press Publishing Assn., 1989), pp. 14–15

360. Lee Boothby

The influences of the anticult hysteria produce exactly the same result in twentieth century America that they did during the antiwitchcraft trials of the seventeenth century. The problem today is that there are too many Cotton Mathers running to and fro attempting to select those groups that will be persecuted from among those permitted to enjoy the protection of the First Amendment.

"Government as an Instrument for Private Retribution," in Dean M. Kelley, ed.,
Government Intervention in Religious Affairs (1986), p. 105.

361. ———

One searches the history books in vain for names of Americans who are revered today because they used the power of government to plague or destroy an unorthodox or unpopular religious group. It is impossible to find one nation that has risen to true greatness because it rid itself of a despised religious sect. Those who have exterminated the disfavored few have always failed in the end.

Ibid., p. 106

362. Justice William J. Brennan

Religious conflict can be the bloodiest and cruelest conflicts that turn people into fanatics.

Interview with National Public Radio, January 29, 1987

363. Edmund Burke

Religious persecution may shield itself under the guise of a mistaken and overzealous piety.

Address, February 17, 1788

364. Nicholas Murray Butler

Persecution on racial and religious grounds has absolutely no place in a nation given over to liberty.

New York Times (October 8, 1941)

365. Daniel Defoe

And of all the plagues with which mankind are cursed ecclesiastic tyranny's the worst.

The True-Born Englishman, Part 2

366. James M. Dunn, Executive Director of the Baptist Joint Committee, 1981–1999

Theocracy is organized arrogance.

Truth with the Bark on It: The Wit and Wisdom of James M. Dunn
(Washington, D.C.: Baptist Joint Committee, n.d.), p. 20

367. *Fresno* (Calif.) *Bee*

The framers of the Constitution recognized that in a pluralistic society, any state involvement in religion, as promoter or regulator, can be a source of irreconcilable tensions, if not violence.

Editorial, December 5, 1985

368. Cardinal James Gibbons

Our Catholic forefathers suffered so much during the last three centuries for the sake of liberty of conscience that they would rise to condemn us if we made ourselves the advocates of religious persecution.

Address, 1887, quoted in Henry Kamen, *The Rise of Toleration*
(New York: World Universal Library, 1967), p. 241

369. Rev. William R. Harper, Curate of St. John's Episcopal Church, Larchmont, N.Y.

The majority has no right to impose its religion on the rest. That's a tradition as sacred as the Constitution itself to this country.

Gannett Westchester newspaper, December 20, 1986

370. Balthasar Huebmaier, Sixteenth-century Anabaptist

The slayers of the heretics are the worst heretics of all.

1524 declaration

371. President Thomas Jefferson

Certainly, no power to prescribe any religious exercise, or to assume authority in religious discipline, has been delegated to the General Government.

Letter to the Rev. Samuel Miller, January 23, 1808

372. ⸺

Is uniformity attainable? Millions of innocent men, women, and children, since the introduction of Christianity, have been burnt, tortured, fined, imprisoned; yet we have not advanced one inch towards uniformity. What has been the effect of coercion? To make one half the world fools and the other half hypocrites.

Notes on the State of Virginia, 1784

373. John L. Kane, U.S. District Judge

Religious oppression is older than the pyramids of Egypt and as current as the butchering of members of the Bahai faith in Iran today. One of the dominant themes of human history, religious intolerance, unhappily continues with the ferocity and relentlessness of all that is evil in the human spirit.

The Founding Fathers meant to sever religion and government, the better that the people could achieve their secular purpose through the government and their religious purpose through independent churches.

If my right to practice my religion is diminished, then so is yours. If your right to be free from supporting mine is traduced, then so is mine.

Address, Denver, Colo., June 1987

374. Sen. Edward M. Kennedy (D-Mass.)

I hope for an America where the power of faith will always burn brightly, but where no modern Inquisition of any kind will ever light the fires of fear, coercion, or angry division.

Address, Liberty University, Lynchburg, Va., October 3, 1983

375. Frances Kissling, President, Catholics for a Free Choice

From a human rights perspective, it is particularly troubling to see the extent to which secular governments will bend to the will of powerful religious bodies, primarily those that hold conservative views of women.

Address, British House of Lords, January 1996

376. ———

The human rights community must recognize the need to treat the question of religious persecution more broadly. This means addressing not only the legal dimension of human rights . . . but also standing with women of faith in their work to ensure that human rights are honored within religions as well as in the secular world.

Ibid.

377. Ninan Koshy

Promoting religious harmony is one important way to contribute to peace. Today, one major threat to peace comes from violations of religious liberty and intolerance on the basis of religion and belief.

Religious Freedom in a Changing World (Geneva: WCC Publications, 1992), p. 115.
Ninan Koshy was director of the World Council of Churches' Commission
on International Affairs from 1981 to 1991.

378. Douglas Laycock

One lesson of religious persecutions is that the Free Exercise Clause must protect religiously motivated conduct, as well as belief and speech. Conscientious objectors to government policy are willing to suffer greatly rather than violate their conscience; attempts to coerce religious conscience lead inevitably to persecution.

"Original Intent," from The First Freedom: Religion and the Bill of Rights, ed. by James E. Wood Jr.
(Waco, Tex.: J. M. Dawson Institute of Church-State Studies, 1990), p. 106.

379. William E. H. Lecky

Almost all Europe, for many centuries, was inundated with blood, which was shed at the direct instigation or with the full approval of the ecclesiastical authorities.

History of the Rise and Influence of the Spirit of Rationalism in Europe
(New York: Appleton, 1866), vol. 2, p. 32

380. Robert E. Lee

Is it not strange that the descendants of those Pilgrim Fathers who crossed the Atlantic to preserve their own freedom of opinion have always proved themselves intolerant of the spiritual liberty of others?

Letter to his wife, December 27, 1856

381. President James Madison

Torrents of blood have been spilt in the world in vain attempts of the secular arm to extinguish religious discord, by proscribing all differences in religious opinions.

Joseph L. Blau, *Cornerstones of Religious Freedom in America* (Boston: Beacon Press, 1949), p. 85

382. ———

That diabolical, hell-conceived principle of persecution rages among some, and to their eternal infamy the clergy can furnish their quota of imps for such a business.

Ibid.

383. Sidney E. Mead, Historian

When Christians accepted the alliance with Constantine and the Roman Empire, evil because it made Jesus' kingdom-not-of-this-world the tool of very this-worldly empires, they reverted to the old principle of coercion. In doing so they repeated the fatal error so often condemned by the Jewish prophets of putting their hope for salvation in alliances with the militarily powerful. At that point "Christendom" was born, and thereafter, contrary to their true principle, for fourteen centuries with spectacular pomp and circumstance, they depended on violence and coercion, purportedly to build and maintain the kingdom of the one they worshipped as the Prince of Peace. . . .

It was that fourteen centuries of Western history, smeared with the blood of those who consciously or inadvertently deviated from the current orthodoxy, that those we call the founders of the Republic confronted, successfully attacked, and launched "the first new nation" in Christendom. It was "new" because where religion was concerned it was launched on what seems to have been the pre-Christendom Christian principle of sole dependence on the sword of the Spirit, the Word of God. . . .

Because from the sectarian's perspective religion is an all-or-nothing matter, there can be no neutrality where his species of orthodoxy is concerned. Therefore it is impossible for him to conceive of a religiously neutral civil authority. If it is not overtly "Christian" according to his sectarian definition it perforce must be "infidel," "atheist," "godless," or, as the sophisticated now commonly say, "secular." Jefferson had such sectarians in mind when he complained that "They wish it to be believed that he can have no religion who advocates its freedom."

The Old Religion in the Brave New World (Berkeley: University of California Press, 1977), pp. 39–41

384. John Stuart Mill

The liberty of conscience, which above all other things ought to be to all men dearest and most precious . . .

The Ready and Easy Way to Establish a Free Commonwealth
(New Haven: Conn.: Yale University Press, 1915), p. 36

385. Blaise Pascal

Men never do evil so completely and cheerfully as when they do it from religious conviction.

Quoted in Sam J. Ervin Jr., *Preserving the Constitution* (Charlottesville, Va.: Michie, 1984)

386. William Shakespeare

It is a heretic that makes the fire, not she which burns in it.

The Winter's Tale, Act 2, Scene 3

387. Paul D. Simmons

Fanaticism in the name of religion seems to be the great temptation of the age. It is religion without integrity: misled, misguided, angry, insolent, vindictive, hateful, vengeful. It is a crusade in the name of God to rid the earth of all infidels and unbelievers who dare defile the rare atmosphere of heady faith. Dissent is not tolerated. Intelligence is frowned upon unless it is dogmatic and closed. Disturbing questions, clear thinking, and common sense are thought to be irreverent, insolent, and disrespectful of proper authority.

This fanaticism blends politics with religion until basic and important distinctions are blurred. Zealous nationalism takes on the face of fervent religion; patriotism is baptized as kingdom service; love of country is tantamount to love of God and military ventures are regarded as pure paths of martyrdom and Christian service.

Such religion has an ugly face—the scowl of the true believer—the smirk of the conscienceless killer who can do no wrong for it is done in the name of a higher purpose that justifies the wanton act.

Report from the Capital 40 (April 1985): 11

388. ———

Puritanism never dies; it lives to kill the freedom of the human spirit in the name of Christian orthodoxy.

Address, Greenville, Miss., November 6, 1986

389. Sen. Paul Simon (D-Ill.)

Religion is the only field where many leaders assume all truth has been revealed. . . . When people in the name of any religion claim to have the sole possession of truth, they have crossed the line from faith to arrogance. . . .Those who practice rigidity and absolutism in the name of religion, whether simply by word or with arms, will not persuade.

P.S.: the Autobiography of Paul Simon (Chicago: Bonus Books, 1999), pp. 121, 122, 124

390. ———

The Protestants who kill Catholics in Northern Ireland, or the Catholics who kill Protestants, do no favor to their professed faith. Muslim extremists in Algeria who decimate villages cause their faith to be held in ridicule by people around the world. Those who kill have been stimulated by others who preach fanaticism. Religious leaders who advocate with excessive zealotry share the guilt with the murderers who wield the knives and pull the triggers.

Ibid., p. 124

391. Jonathan Swift

We have just enough religion to make us hate, but not enough to make us love one another.

Thoughts on Various Subjects (1711)

392. Voltaire

As you know, the Inquisition is an admirable and wholly Christian invention to make the pope and the monks more powerful and turn a whole kingdom into hypocrites.

Philosophical Dictionary, English translation, 1962

393. Lois Waldman

Most Jews intuitively know that if the evangelical right succeeds in Christianizing America, Jews will again find themselves an isolated minority alien to American culture.

"After Pawtucket," American Jewish Congress, July 1985

394. President George Washington

Of all the animosities which have existed among mankind, those which are caused by a difference of sentiments in religion appear to be the most inveterate and distressing, and ought to be deprecated.

Letter to Edward Newenham, October 20, 1792

RELIGIOUS TESTS FOR PUBLIC OFFICE

395. President Calvin Coolidge

The fundamental precept of liberty is toleration. We cannot permit any inquisition either within or without the law or apply any religious test to the holding of office. The mind of America must be forever free.

Inaugural Address, March 4, 1925

396. Oliver Ellsworth
(Later Chief Justice of the United States)

The sole purpose and effect of it [Article VI] is to exclude persecution and to secure the important right of religious liberty.

Philip B. Kurland and Ralph Lerner, eds., The Founder's Constitution,
(Chicago: University of Chicago Press, 1987), vol. 4, p. 638

397. ———

Legislatures have no right to set up an inquisition and examine into the private opinions of men. Test-laws are useless and ineffectual, unjust and tyrannical.

Ibid., p. 642

398. Jacob Henry

If a man fulfills the duties of that religion, which his education or his conscience has pointed to him as the true one, no person, I hold, in this our land of liberty has a right to arraign him at the bar of any inquisition.

Address to North Carolina Legislature, 1809

399. Sen. Edward M. Kennedy (D-Mass.)

Respect for conscience is most in jeopardy and the harmony of our diverse society is most at risk when we reestablish, directly or indirectly, a religious test for public office.

Address, Liberty University, Lynchburg, Va., October 3, 1983

400. President John F. Kennedy

Voters are more than Catholics, Protestants, or Jews. They make up their minds for many diverse reasons, good and bad. To submit the candidates to a religious test is unfair enough—to apply it to the voters is divisive, degrading, and wholly unwarranted.

Address, American Society of Newspaper Editors, April 21, 1960

401. ———

I believe the American people are more concerned with a man's views and abilities than with the church to which he belongs. I believe the founding fathers meant it when they provided in Article VI of the Constitution that there should be no religious test for public office. And I believe that the American people mean to adhere to those principles today.

Ibid.

402. ———

I would not look with favor upon a President working to subvert the First Amendment's guarantees of religious liberty. . . . Neither do I look with favor upon those who would work to subvert Article VI of the Constitution by requiring a religious test—even by indirection.

Ibid.

403. Thomas Kennedy

There are few Jews in the United States; in Maryland there are very few. But if there were only one—to that one, we ought to do justice.

Address urging a change in the Maryland State Constitution clause
that required officials to declare their belief in Christianity, 1823.

404. President James Knox Polk

Thank God, under our Constitution there was no connection between Church and State, and that in my action as President of the United States I recognized no distinction of creeds in my appointments to office.

George Seldes, *The Great Quotations* (New York: Lyle Stuart, 1960), p. 169

405. Edmund Randolph

A man of abilities and character, of any sect whatever, may be admitted to any office of public trust under the United States.

In an address to the Virginia Ratifying Convention, June 10, 1788.
The Founders' Constitution, Philip B. Kurland and Ralph Lerner, eds.
(Chicago: University of Chicago Press, 1987), vol. 4, p. 644

406. President Theodore Roosevelt

I believe that this Republic will endure for many centuries. If so there will doubtless be among its Presidents Protestants and Catholics, and very probably at some time, Jews. I have consistently tried while President to act in relation to my fellow Americans of Catholic faith as I hope that any future President who happens to be Catholic will act towards his fellow Americans of Protestant faith. Had I followed any other course I should have felt that I was unfit to represent the American people.

In my Cabinet at the present moment there sit side by side Catholic and Protestant, Christian and Jew, each man chosen because in my belief he is peculiarly fit to exercise on behalf of all our people the duties of the office to which I have appointed him. In no case does the man's religious belief in any way influence his discharge of his duties, save as it makes him more eager to act justly and uprightly in his relations to all men. The same principles that have obtained in appointing the members of my Cabinet, the highest officials under me, the officials to whom is entrusted the work of carrying out all the important policies of my administration, are the principles upon which all good Americans should act in choosing, whether by election or appointment, the man to fill any office from the highest to the lowest in the land.

Letter to J. C. Martin, November 9, 1908

407. ———

To discriminate against a thoroughly upright citizen because he belongs to some particular church, or because, like Abraham Lincoln, he has not avowed his allegiance to any church, is an outrage against that liberty of conscience which is one of the foundations of American life.

Ibid.

408. ———

If there is one thing for which we stand in this country, it is for complete religious freedom, and it is an emphatic negation of this right to cross-examine a man on his religion before being willing to support him for office.

Ibid.

409. ———

Any political movement directed against any body of our fellow-citizens because of their religious creed is a grave offense against American principles and American institutions. It is a wicked thing either to support or oppose a man because of the creed he professes. This applies to Jew and Gentile, to Catholic and Protestant, and to the man who would be regarded as unorthodox by all of them alike. Political movements directed against men because of their religious belief, and intended to prevent men of that creed from holding office, have never accomplished anything but harm. Such a movement directly contravenes the spirit of the Constitution itself. Washington and his associates believed that it was essential to the existence of this Republic that there should never be any union of Church and State; and such union is partially accomplished whenever a given creed is aided by the State or when any public servant is elected or defeated because of his creed. The Constitution explicitly forbids the requiring of any religious test as a qualification for holding office. To impose such a test by popular vote is as bad as to impose it by law. To vote either for or against a man because of his creed is to impose upon him a religious test and is a clear violation of the spirit of the Constitution.

Address, Carnegie Hall, October 12, 1915

410. Justice Joseph Story

This clause [Article VI, U.S. Constitution] is not introduced merely for the purpose of satisfying the scruples of many respectable persons, who feel an invincible repugnance to any religious test, or affirmation. It had a higher object; to cut off forever every pretense of any alliance between church and state in the national government. The framers of the Constitution were fully sensible of the dangers from this source, marked out in the history of other ages and countries;

and not wholly unknown to our own. They knew that bigotry was unceasingly vigilant in its stratagems to secure to itself an exclusive ascendancy over the human mind; and that intolerance was ever ready to arm itself with all the terrors of the civil power to exterminate those who doubted its dogmas, or resisted its infallibility. The Catholic and the Protestant had alternately waged the most ferocious and unrelenting warfare on each other. . . . The history of the parent country, too, could not fail to instruct them in the uses and the abuses of religious tests. They there found the pains and penalties of nonconformity written in no equivocal language and enforced with a stern and vindictive jealousy.

Philip B. Kurland and Ralph Lerner, eds., *The Founder's Constitution*
(Chicago: University of Chicago Press, 1987), vol. 4, p. 638

411. United States Constitution, Article VI

No religious test shall ever be required as a qualification to any office or public trust under the United States.

SCHOOL PRAYER

412. Robert S. Alley

Only little more than four years after the 1962 Engel decision, the evidence was growing that advocates of public school prayers and Bible reading were readily prepared to persecute citizens who dared to challenge the old ways of a presumed Protestant Establishment. Sadly, as we survey the national landscape in the year 1996, we find that those citizens who have sought to implement the Bill of Rights in public schools against the prevailing cultural mores continue to suffer discrimination.

Without a Prayer: Religious Expression in Public Schools
(Amherst, N.Y.: Prometheus Books, 1996), pp. 17–18

413. American Lutheran Church

Laws mandating "voluntary" prayer in the public schools are unnecessary. Moreover, were the state to mandate such prayer, it would be no longer genuinely voluntary. . . . Devotional exercises to cultivate and nurture the religious faith of young people do not belong in the schools, but in the home and the church.

Resolution adopted October 1984

414. *Atlanta Constitution*

Americans can rest assured that their right to pray, each according to his own belief and conscience, is just as firmly guaranteed today as it was when the founding fathers wrote the Constitution and provided for the separation of church and state and for religious freedom.

Editorial, November 9, 1971, hailing the defeat of the Wylie Prayer Amendment
in the U.S. House of Representatives.

415. Rep. Sherwood Boehlert (R-N.Y.)

The Religious Freedom Amendment has nothing to do with expanding religious freedom, and everything to do with expanding the opportunities for religious coercion. The Religious Freedom Amendment has nothing to do with praying for people's betterment, and everything to do with preying on people's darker instincts—their fear, their prejudice, their lack of knowledge of the state of American law.

Address, U.S. House of Representatives, June 4, 1998. Mr. Boehlert was expressing his opposition to
a school prayer constitutional amendment, misleadingly called the Religious Freedom Amendment,
proposed by Oklahoma Republican Representative Ernest Istook. The Istook proposal was defeated.

416. President Jimmy Carter

The government ought to stay out of the prayer business.

Press Conference, Washington, D.C., 1979

417. Stephen L. Carter

By choosing among possible prayers, and then forcing its choice on impression-able children who look to their schools for guidance, the state in effect coerces religious adherence. . . . The powers of the state should not be used to coerce religious belief, and it's impossible to design a noncoercive approach to school prayer.

The Culture of Disbelief (New York: Basic Books, 1993), p. 188

418. Sen. Sam J. Ervin Jr. (D-N.C.)

A school prayer amendment would confer upon public school boards a power the First Amendment now denies to Congress and the states, that is, the power to establish religion.

Preserving the Constitution (Charlottesville, Va.: Michie, 1984)

419. Joe Loconte

A growing number of conservative, evangelical Christians are raising deep concerns about the difficulties that even student-led prayer creates in matters of faith, conscience, and civility. School prayer was not the glue that held together a moral or religious consensus in society; neither will its return lead to spiritual or cultural renewal. Religious conservatives ought to be the first to raise objections when spiritual disciplines like prayer are reduced to public exercises to help ward off social ills. America's growing cultural pluralism makes school prayer an anachronistic proposition; it assumes a religious consensus that almost all evangelicals admit no longer exists. In such an environment, children of minority faiths or of no faith will endure the subtle intimidation of a majority-ridden benediction.

Policy Review (winter 1995)

420. Rabbi Daniel Polish

The public schools of this country serve the admirable function of bringing together on common ground students from a diversity of cultural and religious backgrounds. The introduction of public prayer into such a setting jeopardizes the sense of community and unnecessarily intrudes an emotional and divisive factor.

Testimony on behalf of the Synagogue Council of America,
September 8, 1980, U.S. House of Representatives

SECULAR STATE

421. Americans for Religious Liberty

We believe in the American tradition of religious and intellectual freedom within a secular democratic state. We believe in the philosophy of Thomas Jefferson and

James Madison which gave birth to this tradition. We believe in the American Constitution and the Bill of Rights which makes it the law of the land.

In this time of political, religious, and moral confusion we re-affirm our commitment to this tradition and call upon all Americans to do the same.

A free and secular democratic state guarantees religious liberty. It guarantees equal freedom to the religious and the non-religious. It makes religious faith a private matter and gives no special privileges to any religious idea or practice. Both prayers sponsored by public schools and public aid to private schools are violations of its integrity.

A free and secular democratic state promotes good citizenship. It fosters respect for the law and respect for the rights and dignity of all citizens. It establishes a free and religiously neutral system of public education. It provides for moral instruction in the public schools through the use of reason and common sense. It encourages religious and other private institutions to reinforce these values in accordance with their own religious beliefs.

A free and secular democratic state values education in science. It recognizes that a strong country needs citizens who are trained in the methods of science and makes it available through public institutions. Since it protects the integrity of science and free inquiry it refuses to allow public school classrooms to be used for religious indoctrination. It especially defends the integrity of modern biology. The evolution of life is science. It is more than speculation. It is an established truth, which over one hundred years of biological research has confirmed.

A free and secular democratic state supports intellectual freedom. It encourages free speech and open discussion. It recognizes that creative and useful ideas emerge from controversy. It protects public schools and public libraries from arbitrary censorship.

A free and secular democratic state secures personal freedom and privacy. It defends the individual against the tyranny of transient majorities or determined minorities. It allows all people to follow their own consciences and restrains them only when they harm the public welfare. It makes abortion and sexual behavior between consenting adults issues of personal choice.

A free and secular democratic state provides equal dignity for all. It refuses to place any ethnic, racial, religious, sex, or age limitation on the enjoyment of rights and privileges. It deplores any effort to deny women equal status with men.

A free and secular democratic state defends the independence of its court system. It resists any attempt to strip the courts of their authority to review controversial legislation. It affirms the truth that a good democracy is a constitutional democracy.

A free and secular democratic state is the traditional American guarantee of religious, intellectual, and moral freedom.

In a world where many voices of extremism seek to subvert freedom, we need to be voices of reason and to rally to its support.

Statement of Principles, 1982

422. Edward L. Ericson, Cofounder of Americans for Religious Liberty

The historic alliance of liberal and evangelical forces, joined in support of freedom of thought and the separation of church and state, brought into being and sustains our pluralistic secular democracy. The secular democratic state is the surest protector of religious and intellectual liberty ever crafted by human ingenuity. Nothing is more fallacious, or inimical to genuine religious liberty, than the seductive notion that the state should "favor" or "foster" religion. All history testifies that such practices inevitably result in favoring one religion over less powerful minorities and secular opinion.

In the long run governmental favoritism vitiates the religious spirit itself. Where in the Western world is organized religion stronger than in the United States where the church is a take-your-choice affair? Where is it weaker than in Europe where sophisticated secularists joke that they have been "inoculated" for life against religion by compulsory religious indoctrination in state schools? Preserving the secular character of government and the public school is the surest guarantee that religion in America will remain free, vital, uncorrupted by political power, and independent of state manipulation.

American Freedom and the Radical Right (New York: Frederick Ungar, 1982)

423. William Reed Huntington

Our government rests in theory, and must eventually rest in practice, upon a purely secular basis.

The Church-State Idea (New York: Scribner's, 1899), p. 100.
Huntington was a Episcopalian clergyman and rector of Grace Church in New York.

424. Leo Pfeffer

America has given to the world a precious jewel. It has shown that a government whose concerns are purely secular and which leaves to the individual conscience of its citizenry all obligations that relate to God is the one which is actually the most friendly to religion. It is a precious jewel that we have. We should guard it well.

Earl Raab, ed., *Religious Conflict in America* (New York: Anchor, 1964), p. 163

425. John M. Swomley

Equality of all religious bodies before the law is possible only in a secular state.

Religious Liberty and the Secular State (Amherst, N.Y.: Prometheus Books, 1987)

426. James E. Wood Jr., Director of J. M. Dawson Institute of Church-State Studies, Baylor University

The secular state stands as a bulwark for religious liberty in its denial of the state's giving religious means for the accomplishment of political ends. . . . The secular state is one which the church should welcome, since the secular state is not an enemy of religion, but a protector of religious liberty.

Nationhood and the Kingdom (Nashville, Tenn.: Broadman, 1977)

427. ———

The present trend to repudiate the concept of America as a secular state and officially to identify this nation with God and certain sectarian religious views does not bode well for religious pluralism in the United States, in which virtually all of the world's religions are represented among its citizens, along with new religious movements that are making substantial gains. America is a state in which church and synagogue, religion and irreligion are equal before the law and where citizens are neither to enjoy any advantages nor to suffer any disadvantages because of their religion. America is a state which seeks neither to promote nor to hinder the free exercise of religion, in which neither religion nor irreligion is to enjoy any official status or support on the part of the government.

"Religious Pluralism and American Society," in *Ecumenical Perspectives on Church and State,* ed. James E. Wood Jr. (Waco, Tex.: Baylor University Press, 1988), p. 16

428. ———

As a secular state America is a nation in which neither religion nor irreligion enjoys any official status and where no church or religion is to enjoy any advantages or to suffer any disadvantages because of an establishment of religion. Religious identity is made irrelevant to one's right of citizenship, e.g., the right to vote and to hold public office. One's religion or irreligion may not be made the basis of political privilege or discrimination.

Editorial, Journal of Church and State (spring 1987)

SEPARATION OF CHURCH AND STATE

429. James Luther Adams, Theologian, Harvard Divinity School

The demand for the separation of church and state and the emergence of the voluntary church represent the end of an old era and the beginning of a new one. The earlier era had been dominated by the ideal of "Christendom," a unified structure of society in a church-state. In the new era the voluntary church, the free church, no longer supported by taxation, was to be self-sustaining; and it was to manage its own affairs. In the earlier era, kinship, caste, and restricted community groups had determined most of the interests and the forms of participation. In the new era these interests became segregated. In this respect the freedom of choice was increased. The divorce of church and state and the advent of freedom of religious association illustrate this type of increase in freedom of choice.

On Being Human Religiously (Boston: Beacon Press, 1976)

430. Hashem Aghajeri, Iranian Reformer

It is time for the institution of religion to become separated from the institution of government.

Address, Beshesti University, Tehran, July 30, 2000

431. ———

Religion has performed badly when it has been coupled with power.

Ibid.

432. ———

Governments that suppress thinking under the name of religion are not religious governments, but are not even humane governments.

Ibid.

433. American Jewish Congress

The principle of separation of church and state as a foundation of our constitutional system has always meant that religion is outside the recognition and sphere of the political government and that the state has no constitutional power to enter alliances with churches and other religious bodies.

November 19, 1951

434. *Atlanta Constitution*

The framers of the Bill of Rights were right when they foresaw the need to keep church and government interests strictly separate, and that becomes more obvious with each incursion by the uncomfortably parochial Reagan administration. The Founding Fathers understood the dangers: When religion and state embrace, it is the state that gives the bear hug.

Editorial, January 26, 1985

435. Isaac Backus

Religious matters are to be separated from the jurisdiction of the state not because they are beneath the interests of the state, but, quite to the contrary, because they are too high and holy and thus are beyond the competence of the state.

An Appeal to the Public for Religious Liberty (1773)

436. John C. Bennett

The first reason for emphasizing the separation of church and state is that it is the only way of assuring the complete freedom of the church. . . . The second reason for believing in the separation of church and state is the preservation of the state from control by the church. . . . The third reason for emphasizing the separation of church and state is that it is best for the church to be on its own.

Christians and the State (New York: Charles Scribner's Sons, 1958)

437. Jeremiah S. Black, Chief Justice of the Pennsylvania Supreme Court

The manifest object of the men who framed the institutions of this country, was to have a State without religion and a Church without politics—that is to say, they meant that one should never be used as an engine for the purposes of the other. . . . For that reason they built up a wall of complete and perfect partition between the two.

Essays and Speeches (New York: D. Appleton and Co., 1885), p. 53

438. Joseph L. Blau

It might be said that religious freedom in the American sense, incorporating the separation of church and state, has been the pivotal concept of the national development of the United States of America.

"The Wall of Separation," *Union Seminary Quarterly Review* 38 (1984): 283

439. Lee Boothby

Religion separated from the political control of the state can be a powerful force for public good. But religion used by the state to further its political purposes will ultimately destroy the state and compromise the effectiveness of the church.

"Healing the Hurts of the Past," *The Role of the Churches in the Renewing Societies* (Lectures and Documents—Budapest Symposium), March 3–5, 1997, pp. 35–36

440. James Bryce

It is accepted as an axiom by all Americans that the civil power ought to be not only neutral and impartial as between different forms of faith, but ought to leave these matters entirely on one side, regarding them no more than it regards the artistic or literary pursuits of the citizens.

The American Commonwealth, vol. 2, 1888, p. 766

441. Leonard Busher

Kings and magistrates are to rule temporal affairs by the swords of their temporal kingdoms, and bishops and ministers are to rule spiritual affairs by the Word and Spirit of God, the sword of Christ's spiritual kingdom, and not to intermeddle one with another's authority, office, and function. . . . It is not only unmerciful, but unnatural and abominable, yes, monstrous, for one Christian to vex and destroy another for difference and questions of religion.

"Religious Peace or a Plea for Liberty of Conscience," a petition to King James I. Anson Phelps Stokes, *Church and State in the United States* (New York: Harper, 1950), vol. 1, p. 113.

442. R. Freeman Butts

One of the thorniest aspects of the first modernization process was the confrontation between establishments of religion and those seeking separation of church and state. The establishments of religion were looked upon as citadels of the traditional standing orders that had to be stormed if the forces of modernity were to be victorious. The political struggles over disestablishment were constant, severe, and often debilitating. Only in the United States was a reasonably clear-cut victory won for the separation of church and state. This was undoubtedly one of the reasons why the United States was able to forge ahead so rapidly in its modernization. There were no enormously powerful land-owning churches to hold off political reform or economic development as they did in Eastern and Southern Europe, and for a time in France, England, and Germany.

But it also turned out that political action based upon a secular theory of natural rights was not the only, perhaps not even the most important, aspect of the disestablishment process. The political role of noncomformist, dissenting churches, or radical Protestant sects who believed in the free exercise of religion without interference by government in religious creed or practice proved to be indispensable. "Separatists" like the Quakers, Baptists, Methodists, and Mennonites were opposed to establishments of religion on principle, but even those who were believers in a close alliance between church and state (Presbyterian, Congregationalist, Lutheran, Catholic) began to see the values of separation in societies where they were not the dominant church. Thus, the religious heterogeneity of the American colonies helped to undermine the religious establishments which had benefited from laws that imposed the doctrines of the preferred church and taxes that were levied upon everyone for the support of the established clergy.

The Education of the West (New York: McGraw-Hill, 1973), p. 304

443. President Jimmy Carter

I believe in the separation of church and state and would not use my authority to violate this principle in any way.

Letter to Jack V. Harwell, August 11, 1977, Box RM1, White House Central Files, Jimmy Carter Library

444. Stephen L. Carter

Church-state separation is the durable and vital doctrine that shields our public institutions from religious domination and our religious institutions from government domination.

The Culture of Disbelief (New York: Basic Books, 1993), p. 6

445. *Chicago Tribune*

The principle of church-state separation may sometimes be inconvenient or costly to one side or the other. But there is one great thing about that wall: it works for both sides.

Editorial, June 12, 1985

446. *Christian Science Monitor*

Overriding all other considerations is the wise foresight of the framers of the Constitution in ensuring the freedom of religion by keeping the state out of it.

Editorial opposing tuition tax credits, February 26, 1973

447. Henry Clay

All religions united with government are more or less inimical to liberty. All, separated from government, are compatible with liberty.

Address, U.S. House of Representatives, March 24, 1818

448. DeWitt Clinton, Governor of New York

In this country there is no alliance between church and state, no established religion, no tolerated religion—for toleration results from establishment—but religious freedom guaranteed by the Constitution and consecrated by the social compact.

1813

449. President Bill Clinton

I have a deep belief that the First Amendment separation between church and state is what guarantees the religious freedom of all people.

Campaign address, South Bend, Ind., September 1992

450. Henry Steele Commager, Historian

[T]he decision for complete religious freedom and for separation of church and state in the eyes of the rest of the world [was] perhaps the most important decision reached in the New World. Everywhere in the western world of the eighteenth century, church and state were one; and everywhere the state maintained an established church and tried to force conformity to its dogma.

The British had attempted—half-heartedly—to extend the Anglican Establishment to America, but they had, on the whole, permitted a good deal of religious freedom and independence. When the American states became independent they inevitably threw off the Anglican Establishment. A few of them tried to keep an establishment of their own, but given the pluralism of American religion, that attempt was clearly foredoomed.

Virginia led the way by announcing not only complete religious freedom, but the separation of church and state, and thereafter, one after another, all the original states followed this principle. When James Madison introduced the Bill of Rights to the first Congress, the very first of them embraced freedom of religion, and that was adopted by the Congress and by the states, and incorporated as a fundamental article of American constitutionalism.

Thus the new United States took the lead among the nations of the earth in the establishment of religious freedom. That is one reason America has never had any religious wars or any religious persecutions.

Modern Maturity (June–July 1976)

451. Isaac Cornelison

Christianity does not need the fostering of the state.

The Relation of Religion to Civil Government (New York: 1895), p. 345.
Reprinted by DaCapo Press, 1970.

452. Cardinal Richard Cushing, Archbishop of Boston

I don't know of anywhere in the history of Christianity where the Catholic Church, the Protestant Church, or any other church has made greater progress than in the United States of America; and in my opinion the chief reason is that there is no union of church and state.

Boston Globe (January 26, 1964)

453. Cardinal Cahal B. Daly, Primate of Ireland

It is for the good of both religion and politics that the spheres of both be clearly distinguished. The churches must not act as spokespersons for political parties or as proxies for political leaders.

The Price of Peace (Belfast: Blackstaff Press, 1991), p. 248

454. Derek H. Davis

In a properly functioning liberal democracy, government stays out of the religious lives of its citizens not because it is antagonistic or even indifferent to religion, but because of society's commitment to allowing its citizens to choose for themselves how they will live and believe. Liberal democracy recognizes that any attempt by government to enforce belief—no matter how innocuous—is an incremental erosion of the individual's freedom of conscience.

"Religion and the Abuse of Judicial Power,"
Journal of Church and State 39 (spring 1997): 206

455. ———

Religious exercises in the courtroom not only lend the government's coercive powers to religion and potentially send a message of disenfranchisement to those outside the judge's religion, they also risk conveying a message of divine imprimatur upon the proceedings themselves.

Ibid., p. 209

456. James M. Dunn, Executive Director of the Baptist Joint Committee, 1981–1999

The best thing government can do for religion is to leave it alone.

Report from the Capital (October 1983)

457. ———

We are seeing in the United States today a deliberate attempt to collapse the distinction between mixing politics and religion (which is inevitable) and merging church and state (which is inexcusable).

Report from the Capital (October 1984).

458. Cynthia Dwyer

I learned how valuable our Constitution is and how valuable the separation of church and state is.

Statement, February 1981. Ms. Dwyer was an American hostage held in Iran.

459. Bishop John England, Catholic bishop of Charleston, S.C., 1820–1842

The United States is a country of no distinct religious denomination, but one of perfect freedom, and of a vast variety of religious opinions; one whose inhabitants have solemnly interdicted to its government any interference, direct or indirect, with the subject of their religion.

Letter, September 19, 1831, *The Works of the Right Rev. John England* (Baltimore: John Murphy & Co., 1849)

460. ———

Our federal government is not warranted to intermeddle with the interests of religion, directly or indirectly. It is not commissioned to take any part whatever in religious concerns.

Letter, September 26, 1831. Ibid.

461. President James Garfield

The divorce between church and state should be absolute.

Quoted in Paul Blanshard, *God and Man in Washington* (Boston: Beacon Press, 1960), p. 226

462. Cardinal James Gibbons

American Catholics rejoice in our separation of Church and State, and I can conceive no combination of circumstances likely to arise which would make a union desirable to either Church or State. We know the blessings of our arrangement; it gives us liberty and binds together priests and peoples in a union better than Church and State.

North American Review (March 1909)

463. Gioberti

The absolute separation of the spiritual from the temporal is about to be established among the most civilized peoples.

Quoted in S. William Halperin, *The Separation of Church and State in Italian Thought from Cavour to Mussolini* (Chicago: University of Chicago Press, 1937), p. 115

464. Parke Godwin, Essayist and Son-in-law of William Cullen Bryant

Our fathers, with a wisdom as divine as was ever vouchsafed to any conclave or synod, decreed an eternal separation of church and state. They forbade the use of religious tests in the decision of civil rights, and that prohibition is sound in spirit as well as letter. We hope the American people will never depart from it.

Political Essays, 1856

465. Roland R. Hegstad, Editor, *Liberty* Magazine

Our forefathers did not erect the wall of separation because they were irreligious, but because they were religious. They saw the wall of separation as a wall of protection for both church and state. . . .

They wrote our Constitution against the backdrop of European church-state conflict that had ravaged the Continent for centuries. It is no wonder that they said, "Enough of cooperation of church and state; for the sake of both, for the sake of free men, let us have separation."

And so they built a wall. . . .

Address, October 1966

466. Humanist Manifesto II

The separation of church and state and the separation of ideology and state are imperatives. The state should encourage maximum freedom for different moral, political, religious, and social values in society. It should not favor any particular religious bodies through the use of public monies, nor espouse a single ideology and function thereby as an instrument of propaganda or oppression, particularly against dissenters.

1973

467. Humanist Manifesto 2000

Humanists everywhere have defended the separation of church and state. We believe that the state should be *secular*, neither for nor against religion. We thus reject theocracies that seek to impose one moral or religious code on everyone.

(Amherst, N.Y.: Prometheus Books, 2000)

468. Edward Frank Humphrey

Separation of Church and State is one of America's greatest contributions to modern religion and politics. The adoption of this as a political principle marks an epoch in the history of mankind. Previously at least half the wars of Europe and half the internal troubles since the founding of Christianity had a religious basis. America put an end to religious wars: for herself through the acts of the period on constitution-making; for the world at large through the power of the example thus set.

· *Nationalism and Religion in America* (Boston: Chipman Law, 1924), p. 359

469. William Reed Huntington

The experiment of greatest moment now in progress here is . . . the mutual independence of church and state. We have dissolved a partnership which for fifteen hundred years the world held sacred.

The Church-State Idea (New York: Scribner's, 1899), p. 94

470. President Thomas Jefferson

Believing with you that religion is a matter which lies solely between man and his God, that he owes account to none other for his faith or his worship, that the legislative powers of government reach actions only, and not opinions, I contemplate with sovereign reverence that act of the whole American people which declared that their legislature should "make no law respecting an establishment of religion, or prohibiting the free exercise thereof," thus building a wall of separation between church and state.

Letter to Danbury Baptist Association, January 1, 1802

471. ———

I consider the government of the United States as interdicted by the Constitution from intermeddling with religious institutions. . . . I do not believe it is for the interest of religion to invite the civil magistrate to direct its exercises, its discipline, or its doctrine.

Letter to the Rev. Samuel Miller, January 23, 1808.
Anson Phelps Stokes, *Church and State in the United States* (New York: Harper, 1950), vol. 1, p. 88.

472. President Lyndon B. Johnson

I believe in the American tradition of separation of church and state which is expressed in the First Amendment to the Constitution. By my office—and by personal conviction—I am sworn to uphold that tradition.

Interview, *Baptist Standard*, October 1964

473. Adolph Keller

[T]he experience of nearly every country where church has been separated from state in the past has proven beneficial to the spiritual life of the people.

Protestant Europe: Its Crisis and Outlook (New York: George H. Doran Company, 1927), p. 7

474. President John F. Kennedy

We do not want an official state church. If ninety-nine percent of the population were Catholics, I would still be opposed to it. I do not want civil power combined with religious power. I want to make it clear that I am committed as a matter of deep personal conviction to separation.

Interview, CBS-TV, *Face the Nation*, October 30, 1960

475. ———

It is my firm belief that there should be separation of church and state as we understand it in the United States—that is, that both church and state should be free to operate, without interference from each other in their respective areas of jurisdiction. We live in a liberal, democratic society which embraces wide varieties of belief and disbelief. There is no doubt in my mind that the pluralism which has developed under our Constitution, providing as it does a framework within which diverse opinions can exist side by side and by their interaction enrich the whole, is the most ideal system yet devised by man. I cannot conceive of a set of circumstances which would lead me to a different conclusion.

Letter to Glenn L. Archer, February 23, 1959

476. ———

Whatever one's religion in his private life may be, for the officeholder, nothing takes precedence over his oath to uphold the Constitution and all its parts—including the First Amendment and the strict separation of church and state.

Interview, *Look*, March 3, 1959

477. ———

I believe in an America where the separation of church and state is absolute—where no Catholic prelate would tell the President (should he be Catholic) how to act and no Protestant minister would tell his parishioners for whom to vote—where no church or church school is granted any public funds or political preference—and where no man is denied public office merely because his religion differs from the President who might appoint him or the people who might elect him.

I believe in an America that is officially neither Catholic, Protestant, nor Jewish—where no public official either requests or accepts instructions on public policy from the Pope, the National Council of Churches, or any other ecclesiastical source—where no religious body seeks to impose its will directly or indirectly upon the general populace or the public acts of its officials—and where religious liberty is so indivisible that an act against one church is treated as an act against all.

Address to the Ministerial Association of Greater Houston, September 12, 1960

478. Lucy Killea, California Legislator

I believe in separation of church and state. I cannot as a public official impose my religious views on people who do not share those views.

Address, San Diego, November 1989

479. Max Lerner

But it remains true that one of the articles of the democratic belief in America is the disbelief in any state church or any equation between membership in a church and membership in the American commonwealth. This distinction is crucial to the idea of religious freedom as Americans have practiced it.

The issue of religious freedom in America thus goes beyond discrimination and also beyond the pluralism of the sects, to the core principle of the separation of church and state, as embodied in the constitutional prohibition against any "establishment of religion." Given the experience of Europe as well as that of the early Puritan settlers, the generation of Madison's famous *Remonstrance* saw that an official recognition of a "religious establishment" would hamper religious freedom.

America as a Civilization (New York: Simon & Schuster, 1957), p. 713

480. Leonard W. Levy

The wall of separation ensures the government's freedom from religion and the individual's freedom of religion.

The Establishment Clause: Religion and the First Amendment (New York: Macmillan, 1986)

481. John Locke

I esteem it above all things necessary to distinguish exactly the business of civil government from that of religion and to settle the just bounds that lie between the one and the other.

A Letter Concerning Toleration, 1689

482. ———

As the magistrate has no power to impose by his laws the use of any rites and ceremonies in any church, so neither has he any power to forbid the use of such rites and ceremonies as are already received, approved, and practised by any church; because if he did so, he would destroy the church itself; the end of whose institution is only to worship God with freedom, after its own manner.

Anson Phelps Stokes, *Church and State in the United States* (New York: Harper, 1950), vol. 1, p. 144

483. Rev. C. Stanley Lowell

From the days of ancient Egypt until now the interlocking of church and state has been one of the most prolific sources of mankind's ills. Both church and state have suffered immeasurably from this relationship, but the people themselves have been the principal victims.

It was the genius of the American founding fathers to detect this flaw in the all but universal pattern of church-state relationships. Their determination to separate church and state was the direct result of this discovery.

The Great Church-State Fraud (Washington, D.C.: Robert Luce, 1973), p. 7

484. President James Madison

Every new and successful example of a perfect separation between ecclesiastical and civil matters is of importance.

Letter to Edward Livingston, July 10, 1822

485. Jacques Maritain et al.

It is not the function of the state either to dominate or to control consciences. The Creeds which, in the present state of religious disunity, share souls' allegiance should be free to establish their rites, to preach their teachings, to shape souls, to exercise their apostolate, without the civil authority's mixing into their proper province.

Manifesto, "In the Face of the World's Crisis," signed by eight prominent European Catholics, including Sigrid Undset, Sir Philip Gibbs, and Alfred Noyes, in *Commonweal* 36 (1942): 418–19.

486. *Memphis Commercial Appeal*

Responsibility for religious training rightly rests not with public education but with the family and the religious organization of its choice. Religion in America is strong and free because our founding fathers had the wisdom to separate church and state.

Editorial, July 30, 1980

487. Thomas Paine

As to religion, I hold it to be the indispensable duty of all government to protect all conscientious professors thereof, and I know of no other business which government hath to do therewith.

Common Sense, 1776

488. Leo Pfeffer

Probably ever since the institutions of religion and of secular powers were recognized as separate and distinct in human history, the two forces have competed for and struggled over human destiny. In this struggle the church has sought to dominate the state and use it as an engine for its purposes, and the state has sought to dominate the church and use it as an engine for its purpose.

During temporary periods of history and in scattered areas, the church has dominated the state; but overwhelmingly in time and place, state has dominated church and used it for its own purposes.

Before the launching of the American experiment, the concept of religious liberty and the separation of church and state was—for all practical purposes—unknown. The experiment embodied in the majestic words, "Congress shall make no law respecting an establishment of religion, or prohibiting the free exercise thereof," was a uniquely American contribution to civilization, and one that the other countries of the world in increasing numbers have emulated and are continuing to emulate.

The principle of separation and freedom was conceived as a unitary principle. Notwithstanding occasional instances of apparent conflict, separation guarantees freedom, and freedom requires separation. The experiences in other countries indicate clearly that religious freedom is most secure where church and state are separated, and least secure where church and state are united.

The principle of separation and freedom was conceived to be as absolute as possible within the limitation of human communal society. Only where they were unavoidably necessary to prevent an immediate and grave danger to the security or welfare of the community were infringements on religious freedom to be justifiable, and only to the smallest extent necessary to avoid the danger. Likewise the separation aspect was conceived to be as absolute as could be achieved, predicated as it was on the concept that religion is outside the jurisdiction of government.

When the constitutional fathers and the generation that adopted the Constitution formalized the concept in the First Amendment, they thereby imposed—and intended to impose—on future generations of Americans in church and state a great moral obligation to preserve their experiment and adhere strictly to the principle they expressed. They were fully familiar with the religious wars, the persecutions, and all the other evils that had inevitably accompanied unions of church and state, and sought forever to keep those evils from our shores.

Since man is imperfect, and does not lose all his imperfection when he enters the service of church or state, there have been deviations from the principle. Religious freedom has on occasions been interfered with, and the separation of church and state has on occasions been impaired. These impairments have incorrectly been urged as evidence that it was not the intent of the framers of the First Amendment that the principle be absolute and the separation complete.

These impairments of the principle of absolute separation have inevitably brought with them, in greater or lesser degree, the very evils that the constitutional fathers sought to keep from the new republic; particularly when the impairments have occurred in the area of public education have the evils of inter-religious disharmony and oppression been manifest.

Nevertheless the American people have by and large been faithful to the obligation placed on them by the framers of the First Amendment; church and state have been kept separate, and religious freedom has been preserved. The people have willingly kept faith; whenever an opportunity has presented itself to obtain an expression of the voice of the people, that voice has clearly been expressed on the side of absolute separation and freedom.

Under this system of the separation of church and state and religious freedom, religion has achieved in the United States a high estate unequalled anywhere else in the world. History has justified the great experiment, and has proved the proposition on which it was based—that complete separation of church and state is best for church and best for state, and secures freedom for both.

Church, State & Freedom (Boston: Beacon, 1967), pp. 727–28

489. *Philadelphia Inquirer*

The "wall of separation between church and state" is not a shibboleth. It is a protection of church from state as much as state from church. We respect the position of those who would breach the wall, but we hope the Supreme Court maintains it firmly.

Editorial, November 13, 1972

490. *Pittsburgh Press*

Separation of church and state, even in matters that have no apparent import, is so basic to total freedom that the principle cannot be infringed upon.

Editorial, December 12, 1986

491. Samuel Rabinove

The predominant view of the Jewish community is that all religions will flourish best if government keeps its hands off, neither to hinder nor to help them. Any religion that cannot flourish without governmental assistance, one might suggest, does not deserve to flourish. No religion should be beholden to government, but rather should be free to bear prophetic witness against government, if events so require. Most Jews believe, moreover, that government should not behave as if it is a church or a synagogue, that it should not be performing functions for its citizens that, in their rightful free exercise of religion, they are perfectly capable of performing for themselves without involving either the machinery, the property, or the tax dollars of government. That is why most Jews oppose government subsidy of schools whose chief reason for being is to propagate a religious faith, whether the schools are Jewish, Catholic, Lutheran, Hare Krishna, or whatever. . . .

There has never been absolute separation of church and state in America. But many religions have thrived here in large measure because of general adherence to that principle, despite certain departures from it. The greater the adherence and the fewer the departures, the better it will be for all people of all faiths.

Hence those groups which uphold the separation principle, far from being "ambivalent" toward religion, are actually among its staunchest supporters.

First Things (May 1990)

492. *Rochester Democrat and Chronicle*

A foundation stone of our republic has been the separation of church and state. Unable to preserve that distinction, other countries have deteriorated into unstable theocracies. This must not happen to the United States.

Editorial, April 9, 1967

493. Elihu Root, Secretary of State under Theodore Roosevelt

It is not a question of religion, or of creed, or of party; it is a question of declaring and maintaining the great American principle of eternal separation between Church and State.

Statement Against the Use of Public Funds for Sectarian Education by the State of New York, 1894

494. Carl Sagan

The Bill of Rights decoupled religion from the state, in part because so many religions were steeped in an absolutist frame of mind—each convinced that it alone had a monopoly on the truth and therefore eager for the state to impose this truth on others. Often, the leaders and practitioners of absolutist religions were unable to perceive any middle ground or recognize that the truth might draw upon and embrace apparently contradictory doctrines.

The framers of the Bill of Rights had before them the example of England, where the ecclesiastical crime of heresy and the secular crime of treason had become nearly indistinguishable. Many of the early Colonists had come to America fleeing religious persecution, although some of them were perfectly happy to persecute other people for their beliefs. The Founders of our nation recognized that a close relation between the government and any of the quarrelsome religions would be fatal to freedom—*and* injurious to religion.

The Demon-Haunted World: Science as a Candle in the Dark (New York: Random House, 1995)

495. Rep. Fred Schwengel (R-Iowa)

I believe the strength of the church comes from having to stand on its own. The American idea of separation of church and state makes both stronger and better.
Remarks, National Presbyterian Center, Washington, D.C., December 14, 1971

496. Secular Humanist Declaration

Because of their commitment to freedom, secular humanists believe in the principle of the separation of church and state. The lessons of history are clear: wherever one religion or ideology is established and given a dominant position in the state, minority opinions are in jeopardy. A pluralistic, open, and democratic society allows all points of view to be heard. Any effort to impose an exclusive conception of truth, piety, virtue, or justice upon the whole of society is a violation of free inquiry. Clerical authorities should not be permitted to legislate their own parochial views—whether moral, philosophic, political, educational, or social—for the rest of society.

Nor should tax revenues be exacted for the benefit or support of sectarian religious institutions. Individuals and voluntary associations should be free to accept or not to accept any belief and to support these convictions with whatever resources they may have, without being compelled by taxation to contribute to those religious faiths with which they do not agree. Similarly, church properties should share in the burden of public revenues and should not be exempt from taxation. Compulsory religious oaths and prayers in public institutions (political or educational) are also a violation of the separation principle.

Today, nontheistic as well as theistic religions compete for attention. Regrettably, in communist countries, the power of the state is being used to impose an ideological doctrine on the society, without tolerating the expression of dissenting or heretical views. Here we see a modern secular version of the violation of the separation principle.

Free Inquiry (winter 1980)

497. R. Sargent Shriver, Democratic Candidate for Vice President, 1972

I believe strongly in the Constitutional principle of separating church and state. Our founders were right in fearing that religious freedom would be threatened in the long run by a departure from governmental neutrality in spiritual matters.

Address, New York Avenue Presbyterian Church, Washington, D.C., January 1976

498. Alfred E. Smith, Governor of New York, Democratic Candidate for President, 1928

I believe in absolute freedom of conscience for all men and equality of all churches, all sects, and all beliefs before the law as a matter of right and not as a matter of favor. I believe in the absolute separation of church and state and in the strict enforcement of the Constitution that Congress shall make no law respecting an establishment of religion or prohibiting the free exercise thereof. I believe that no tribunal of any church has any power to make any decree of any force in the law of the land, other than to establish the status of its own communicants within its own church.

Atlantic Monthly (April 1927)

499. John Smyth, The First English Baptist

The magistrate is not by virtue of his office to meddle with religion, or matters of conscience, to force and compel men to this or that form of religion or doctrine.

Confession of Faith, 1611

500. Theodore C. Sorensen

When no one's religion is preferred by the state, everyone's religious liberty is safer. Behind this hospitable, not hostile, wall, the rights of all religious minorities have been secure, and religion as a whole has flourished.

Why I Am a Democrat (New York: Henry Holt, 1996).
The author was a special assistant to President John F. Kennedy.

501. Synagogue Council of America and National Community Relations Council

We regard the principle of separation of church and state as one of the foundations of American democracy. Both political liberty and freedom of religious worship and belief, we are firmly convinced, can remain inviolate only when there exists no intrusion of secular authority in religious affairs or of religious authority in secular affairs. As Americans and as spokesmen for religious bodies, lay and clerical, we therefore deem any breach in the wall separating church and state as jeopardizing the political and religious freedoms that wall was intended to protect.

Amici Curiae, McCollum v. Board of Education, 333 U.S. 203 (1948)

502. Benjamin F. Underwood

There is no argument worthy of the name that will justify the union of the Christian religion with the State. Every consideration of justice and equality forbids it. . . . Every sentiment of honor, every manly feeling, a righteous indignation at injustice, a determination to submit to no religious intolerance, love of peace and the welfare and prosperity of our country, with an ardent and unfaltering attachment to republican institutions—all combine to induce us to demand a separation of Church and State, total and complete, now, henceforth, and forever.

The Practical Separation of Church and State, 1878

503. Unitarian Universalist Association

Whereas, the constitutional principles of religious liberty and the separation of church and state that safeguards liberty, and the ideal of a pluralistic society are under increasing attack in the Congress of the United States, in state legislatures, and in some sectors of the communications media by a combination of sectarian and secular special interests;

Be it resolved: That the 1982 General Assembly of the UUA reaffirms its support for these principles and urges the Board of Trustees and President of the Association, member societies, and Unitarian Universalists in the United States to:

1. Defend the democratic, pluralistic public school, opposing all forms of direct and indirect public aid to support sectarian private schools, such as tuition tax credits or vouchers;

2. Uphold religious neutrality in public education, oppose all government mandated or sponsored prayers, devotional observances, and religious indoctrination in public schools; and oppose efforts to compromise the integrity of public school teaching by the introduction of sectarian religious doctrines, such as "scientific creationism," and by exclusion of educational material on sectarian grounds;

3. Uphold the principle of judicial review, and oppose all efforts to deny the federal courts jurisdiction over school prayer, abortion rights, or other church-state disputes;

4. Uphold the principle enunciated by the U.S. Supreme Court that all levels of government must remain respectfully neutral with regard to all religions;

5. Uphold the constitutional privacy right of every woman, acknowledged by the Supreme Court in 1973 in *Roe* v. *Wade* and other rulings, to plan the number and spacing of her children and to terminate a problem pregnancy in collaboration with her physician, opposing all efforts through legislation or constitutional amendment to restrict that right or to impose by law a "theology of fetal personhood"; and

6. Support all efforts to preserve and strengthen church-state separation.

General Assembly Resolution, June 1982

504. United Presbyterian Church, U.S.A.

The acknowledgment of the place of religion in American life does not justify the mixing of church and state. On religious matters, government must be neutral. . . . The church has no theological ground for laying any claim upon the state for special favors.

Resolution, 1962 General Assembly

505. J. Brent Walker

Our founders understood that, for religion to be meaningful, it must be voluntary, freed from government assistance and control.

Statement released on June 29, 1995, in response to the Supreme Court decision in
Rosenberger v. *University of Virginia*. Walker was then–general counsel
for the Baptist Joint Committee on Public Affairs.

506. Josiah Warren

The disconnection of Church and State was a master stroke for freedom and harmony.

Equitable Commerce, 1855

507. *Washington Post*

Public schools, controlled by public boards of education maintained by public funds and open to all the public regardless of race or religion, have served this country magnificently well. They have been usefully supplemented by private schools, privately controlled and maintained, offering special forms of education and indoctrination to pupils with special needs and desires. It would be a misfortune to confuse the two, especially where religion is concerned. For a separation of church from state has been proved by history to be an indispensable condition alike for political liberty and for religious liberty. Let religious teaching remain within the province of homes and churches and private schools. Let secular education remain within the province of governments controlled by the people and open to all the winds of politics.

Editorial, June 21, 1969

508. Sen. Lowell Weicker (R-Conn.)

That wall, embodied in the First Amendment, is perhaps America's most important contribution to political progress on this planet.

Free Inquiry 3 (summer 1983)

509. ———

Here in the United States there is no value more traditional, more central to our way of life, than that of separation of church and state. It is our great gift to the world.

Maverick: A Life in Politics (Boston: Little, Brown and Co., 1995), p. 126

510. ———

No greater mischief can be created than to combine the power of religion with the power of government; history has shown us that time and time again. The union of the two is bad for religion and for government. It gives rise to tyrants and inquisitors.

Ibid., p. 118

511. ———

There is no question in my mind that the unique concept of keeping matters ecclesiastical out of our governing is America's greatest contribution to the laws of civilization.

Ibid., p. 8. Weicker was U.S. senator from Connecticut from
1971 to 1989 and governor of that state from 1991 to 1995.

TAXATION AND RELIGION

512. Hanover Presbytery

Neither does the Church of Christ stand in need of a general assessment for its support; and most certain we are persuaded that it would be no advantage, but an injury to the society to which we belong. . . .

1778. Anson Phelps Stokes, *Church and State in the United States*
(New York: Harper, 1950), vol., 1, p. 377

513. President James Madison

Because the bill in reserving a certain parcel of land in the United States for the use of said Baptist Church comprises a principle and a precedent for the appropriation of funds of the United States for the use and support of religious societies, contrary to the article of the Constitution which declares that "Congress shall make no law respecting a religious establishment."

Veto message, February 28, 1811.
Madison vetoed a bill granting public lands to a Baptist Church in Mississippi Territory.

514. Justice Lionel Murphy, High Court of Australia

The purpose of the United States establishment clause was clearly to prevent the recognition of and assistance to religion which plagued European countries over many centuries. The religious wars of ancient times were repeated after the Middle Ages and into modern times. In the United Kingdom the struggle between the contending Catholic and Protestant factions, with the emergence of Presbyterians, Methodists, Quakers, Lollards, and many other religious groups, was a bitter illustration of the attempts of religious factions to get the assistance of the state in propagating their views and if possible, suppressing their rivals. The history has a very important economic aspect. One of the dangers of subsidising religious institutions and granting them financial privileges (such as exemption from income tax, land and municipal rates, sales and other taxes) is that such institutions tend to become extremely wealthy, to aggrandize and to become states within a state. The corrective has often been a more or less violent seizure of the assets of the religious institutions, sometimes by the existing sovereign (as did Henry VIII), sometimes by revolutionary movements, which in many countries have had as one of their main objects the suppression of religious institutions and the seizure of their wealth.

Dissenting opinion in *Attorney-General for Victoria v. the Commonwealth*, 33 A.L.R. 321 at 358 (1981), from *Lionel Murphy: The Rule of Law*, ed. Jean and Richard Ely (Sydney: Akron Press, 1986).

515. Paul D. Simmons

Religion in America has never, does not now, and will not in the future depend upon government subsidies to survive.

Address, Greenville, Miss., November 6, 1986

516. John M. Swomley

When the government aids the religious mission of large religious bodies by subsidizing their schools, hospitals, colleges, public charities, or other activities that are used to inculcate church doctrines, win converts, or establish a foothold in a new community, it taxes the public at large, including religious minorities, to pay for these subsidies. Such taxation forces members of minority religious faiths as well as nonbelievers to make a contribution to the religious mission of churches they do not wish to support. The government subsidies given to large churches build their power and influence as well. These subsidies make possible a large empire of hospitals, colleges and charitable enterprises that reach into local communities to provide a government-supported ministry.

Religious Liberty and the Secular State (Amherst, N.Y.: Prometheus Books, 1987)

517. United States Congress

And it is hereby declared to be the policy of the Government of the United States to make no appropriation of money or property for the purpose of founding, maintaining, or aiding by payment for services, expenses, or otherwise, any church or religious denomination, or any institution or society which is under sectarian or ecclesiastical control. . . .

Appropriation Acts for the District of Columbia in 1896 and 1897.
U.S. Statutes at Large, 39: 936, February 23, 1917.

TOLERANCE

518. Samuel Adams

In regard to religion, mutual toleration in the different professions thereof is what all good and candid minds in all ages have ever practiced, and both by precept and example inculcated on mankind . . .

The Rights of the Colonists, 1771

519. Asoka, King of India, c. 270 B.C.E.

All religions deserve reverence for one reason or another. Reverence for another person's religion improves one's own faith and at the same time honors the religion of other people.

The Eastern Hemisphere by Barry K. Beyer, et al. (New York: Macmillan/McGraw Hill, 1991), p. 438

520. *Christian Science Monitor*

It must be remembered that America is an increasingly pluralistic society, an amalgam of different races, cultures, nationalities, religions. In these conditions

Americans can only be grateful for the Constitution's wisdom of erecting a wall of separation between church and state and leaving religious practice to individual conscience.

Religious tolerance is best safeguarded when the state injects itself the least.

Editorial, October 27, 1980

521. St. John Chrysostom

Christians are not to destroy error by force or violence but should work the salvation of men by perseverance, instruction, and love.

Quoted in M. Searle Bates, *Religious Liberty: An Inquiry*
(New York: International Missionary Council, 1945), p. 138

522. Victor Griffin

Sectarianism and confessionalism have been the curse of Ireland, North and South, for far too long. I want a truly republican and pluralist Ireland. The only way forward for Ireland, North and South, is that of a pluralist society based on tolerance.

Address at Liberty Hall, Dublin, September 2, 1983.
Griffin was dean of St. Patrick's Cathedral (Anglican) in Dublin, Ireland, from 1969 to 1991.

523. President Warren G. Harding

In the experiences of a year of the Presidency, there has come to me no other such unwelcome impression as the manifest religious intolerance which exists among many of our citizens. I hold it to be a menace to the very liberties we boast and cherish.

Address, March 24, 1922

524. Jacob Henry

If a man fulfills the duties of that religion, which his education or his conscience has pointed to him as the true one, no person, I hold, in this our land of liberty has a right to arraign him at the bar of any inquisition.

Address to North Carolina Legislature, 1809

525. Sidney Hook, Philosopher

Religious tolerance has developed more as a consequence of the impotence of religions to impose their dogmas on each other than as a consequence of spiritual humility in the quest for understanding first and last things.

"Religious Liberty From the Viewpoint of a Secular Humanist"
in *Religious Conflict in America*, ed. Earl Raab (New York: Anchor Books, 1964), p. 141

526. ———

To deny me the right to err is therefore to deny me the right to believe.

Ibid., p. 150

527. ———

Religious freedom in an open society has the best prospects of flourishing to the extent that it expresses itself as freedom of religious inquiry.

Ibid.

528. President Herbert Hoover

I come of Quaker stock. My ancestors were persecuted for their beliefs. Here they sought and found religious freedom. By blood and conviction I stand for religious tolerance both in act and in spirit.

The New Day (Stanford, Calif.: Stanford University Press, 1928), p. 36

529. President Thomas Jefferson

I never will, by any word or act, bow to the shrine of intolerance, or admit a right of inquiry into the religious opinions of others.

Letter to Edward Dowse, April 19, 1803

530. President John F. Kennedy

I believe in an America where religious intolerance will someday end—where all men and all churches are treated as equals—where every man has the same right to attend or not attend the church of his choice—where there is no Catholic vote, no anti-Catholic vote, no bloc voting of any kind—and where Catholics, Protestants, and Jews, at both the lay and pastoral level, will refrain from those attitudes of disdain and division which have so often marred their works in the past, and promote instead the American ideal of brotherhood.

Address to the Ministerial Association of Greater Houston, September 12, 1960

531. President Abraham Lincoln

When the Know-Nothings get control, it [the Declaration of Independence] will read: "All men are created equal except negroes, foreigners, and Catholics." When it comes to this I should prefer emigrating to some country where they make no pretense of loving liberty—to Russia, for instance, where despotism can be taken pure, and without the base alloy of hypocrisy.

Letter to Joshua F. Speed, August 24, 1855

532. U.S. District Judge Raymond J. Pettine

Excessive government entanglement with religion can only lead to trouble. Neutrality is the *sine qua non* for a democracy that prizes itself in having a Bill of Rights designed to protect us against despotic abuse of authority by the government. The Constitution is a monumental blessing and its moral guidance in this pluralistic society is its tolerance and understanding for all.

Address, Providence, R.I., 1985

533. President William Howard Taft

There is nothing so despicable as a secret society that is based upon religious prejudice and that will attempt to defeat a man because of his religious beliefs. Such a society is like a cockroach—it thrives in the dark. So do those who combine for such an end.

Address, December 20, 1914

534. President Harry S. Truman

We have gone a long way toward civilization and religious tolerance, and we have a good example in this country. Here the many Protestant denominations, the Catholic Church and the Greek Orthodox Church do not seek to destroy one another in physical violence just because they do not interpret every verse of the Bible in exactly the same way. Here we now have the freedom of all religions, and I hope that never again will we have a repetition of religious bigotry, as we have had in certain periods of our own history. There is no room for that kind of foolishness here.

Mr. Citizen (New York: Bernard Geis, 1960), pp. 98–99

535. Voltaire

Of all religions the Christian is without doubt the one which should inspire tolerance most, although up to now the Christians have been the most intolerant of all men.

Quoted in Harry Elmer Barnes, *An Intellectual and Cultural History of the Western World* (New York: Random House, 1937), p. 766

536. *Washington Post*

The answer lies in the common understanding we have as Americans about our diverse religious views and our respect for each other's beliefs. This tolerance binds us as a people and protects us as individuals. We have agreed that each person may practice his own religion without interference from the state, and we don't want the government to do anything that will promote one religion over another.

Let crèches appear on every church lawn in Rhode Island. Let the Pawtucket merchants association build one out of marble. But keep the city council and the taxpayers' money on the other side of Thomas Jefferson's wall lest an intrusive government, eager to support the large majority, crowd out, separate and impose on others whose rights are sacred too.

Editorial, March 7, 1984

537. Wendell Wilkie, Republican Candidate for President, 1940

I am not interested in the support of anybody who stands for any form of prejudice as to anybody's race or religion. I don't want it. I have no place in my philosophy for such beliefs. I don't have to be President of the United States but I do have to live with myself.

Statement repudiating the endorsement of the anti-Semitic *Social Justice* magazine during the 1940 presidential campaign, August 27, 1940. Gustavus Myers, *History of Bigotry in the United States* (New York: Random House, 1943), p. 413.

538. President Woodrow Wilson

It does not become America that within her borders, where every man is free to follow the dictates of his conscience, men should raise the cry of church against church. To do that is to strike at the very spirit and heart of America.

Address, November 4, 1915

TOLERATION

539. Daniel J. Boorstin

In this United States, for the first time in modern Western history, the nation leaped from the provincial religious preference of its regions into religious liberty for the whole nation. The Founding Fathers despised the condescension that was implied in the very concept of toleration. That was a stage necessary for Old World nations, but not for our New World nation.

"The Founding Fathers and the Courage to Doubt,"in Robert S. Alley, ed.,
James Madison on Religious Liberty (Amherst, N.Y.: Prometheus Books, 1985), p. 209

540. DeWitt Clinton, Governor of New York

In this country there is no alliance between church and state, no established religion, no tolerated religion—for toleration results from establishment—but religious freedom guaranteed by the Constitution and consecrated by the social compact.

1813

541. President Calvin Coolidge

The fundamental precept of liberty is toleration. We cannot permit any inquisition either within or without the law or apply any religious test to the holding of office. The mind of America must be forever free.

Inaugural Address, March 4, 1925

542. John Leland

The liberty I contend for is more than toleration. The very idea of toleration is despicable; it supposes that some have a pre-eminence above the rest to grant indulgence; whereas all should be equally free, Jews, Turks, Pagans, and Christians. Test Oaths and established creeds should be avoided as the worst of evils.

Short Essay on Government, 1820

543. President Franklin D. Roosevelt

The lessons of religious toleration—a toleration which recognizes complete liberty of human thought, liberty of conscience—is one which, by precept and example, must be inculcated in the hearts and minds of all Americans. If the institutions of our democracy are to be maintained and perpetuated.

We must recognize the fundamental rights of man. There can be no true national life in our democracy unless we give unqualified recognition to freedom of religious worship and freedom of education.

Letter to the Calvert Associates, 1937. Samuel I. Rosenman, ed., *The Public Papers and Addresses of Franklin D. Roosevelt* (Washington, D.C.: U.S. Government Printing Office), vol. 4, p. 96

544. President George Washington

It is now no more that toleration is spoken of as if it was by the indulgence of one class of the people that another enjoyed the exercise of their inherent natural rights. For happily the Government of the United States, which gives to bigotry no sanction, to persecution no assistance, requires only that those who live under its protection should demean themselves as good citizens in giving it, on all occasions, their effectual support.

Letter to the congregation of Touro Synagogue, Newport, R.I., August 1790

VATICAN AMBASSADOR AND HOLY SEE AT THE UNITED NATIONS

545. Edd Doerr

Establishment of diplomatic relations with the Holy See is objectionable on constitutional and public policy grounds because:

It has the unconstitutional effect of preferring one religion over all others;

It unconstitutionally creates the potential for excessive government entanglement between our government and a church;

It creates new and exacerbates old tensions between faiths, as the public reactions to this appointment have shown;

It unconstitutionally creates the potential for political division along religious lines;

It implies, in Madison's words, that "the Civil Magistrate . . . may employ Religion as an engine of Civil Policy . . . [which is] an unhallowed pervasion of the means of salvation" ("Memorial and Remonstrance");

It conveys to all Americans the impression that their government values one religion over all others;

It blurs our uniquely American constitutional dividing line between church and state;

It necessitates unconstitutional congressional appropriation or reprogramming of funds for operating an embassy to the Holy See;

By violating the spirit and the letter of the First Amendment, it renders that guarantee of religious liberty more vulnerable to other forms of erosion and attack.

Testimony before the U.S. Senate Subcommittee on
Commerce, Justice, State, the Judiciary, and Related Agencies, March 5, 1984

546. Dean M. Kelley, Executive for Religious Liberty, National Council of Churches

The president's appointment of a full ambassador to the Holy See—an appointment endorsed by the Senate and funded with appropriations initiated by the House—is a clear case of the U.S. government's showing special favor to one particular religious body and not to others. . . . The salient vice of the present appointment is giving privileged access to one particular faith at the expense of others.

How Does the Constitution Protect Religious Freedom? ed. Robert A. Goldwin and Art Kaufman,
(Washington, D.C.: American Enterprise Institute, 1987), pp. 125–26

547. President John F. Kennedy

I am flatly opposed to appointment of an ambassador to the Vatican. Whatever advantages it might have in Rome—and I'm not convinced of these—they would be more than offset by the divisive effect at home.

Look (March 3, 1959)

548. Joanna Manning

The Vatican's obstructive tactics on women's rights at international forums have caused the Catholic Church to lose credibility as a spiritual and moral force in the world.

Quoted by Christopher Shulgan in
"Canadians Join Move to Oust Vatican from UN International Coalition," *National Post* (Canada),
April 19, 1999. Women's rights advocate Manning is author of *Is the Pope Catholic?*

549. Anika Rahman

To ensure that the United Nations does not promote any particular religion, religious entities such as the Roman Catholic Church should not be permitted to participate in this forum as a non-member state.

Remarks at press conference, March 24, 1999.
Rahman is director of international programs at the Center for Reproductive Law and Policy.

550. "See Change"

As a UN Non-member State Permanent Observer, the Holy See enjoys unique status, often as a voting partner, with countries at UN conferences. Granting governmental privileges to what is in reality a religious body is questionable statecraft. While the Holy See—the government of the Roman Catholic Church—has made positive contributions through the United Nations to peace and justice, this should not be used to justify granting the status of a state to a religious institution.

Governmental participation in the UN should be reserved for actual states. The world's religions have been well represented through nongovernmental organization status. With NGO status, the Roman Catholic Church would be able to continue its participation in the UN—like the World Council of Churches—without ambiguity or privilege. We call on you to open an Official review of the Holy See's status at the UN.

Petition to UN Secretary General Kofi Annan from Catholics for a Free Choice and more than
five hundred organizations and tens of thousands of individuals from more than eighty countries.
The "See Change" campaign began in 1999.

VOLUNTARY PRINCIPLE IN RELIGION

551. James Luther Adams,
Theologian, Harvard Divinity School

And then there are the churches. Since the time of separation of church and state they have been classified as voluntary associations: they depend in principle upon voluntary membership and voluntary contributions. The collection plate in the Sunday Service is sometimes objected to for aesthetic reasons, but it is an earnest, indeed a symbol, of the voluntary character of the association, and it should be interpreted in this fashion. It is a way of saying to the community, "This is our voluntary, independent enterprise, and under God's mercy we who believe in it will support it. We do not for its support appeal to the coercive power of the state."

On Being Human Religiously (Boston: Beacon Press, 1976)

552. Athanasius, Bishop of Alexandria

It is not by the sword or the spear, by soldiers or by armed force that truth is to be promoted, but by counsel and gentle persuasion.

Quoted in M. Searle Bates, *Religious Liberty: An Inquiry*
(New York: International Missionary Council, 1945), p. 138

553. Rev. Lyman Beecher, Congregationalist Clergyman

[Disestablishment was] the best thing that ever happened to the state of Connecticut. It cut the churches loose from dependence on state support. It threw them wholly on their own resources and on God.

The Autobiography of Lyman Beecher
(Cambridge: Harvard University Press, 1961 edition), vol. 1, p. 253

554. Monsignor Thomas J. Curry

The people of almost every state that ratified the First Amendment believed that religion should be maintained and supported voluntarily. They saw government attempts to organize and regulate such support as a usurpation of power, as a violation of liberty of conscience and free exercise of religion.

The First Freedoms (New York: Oxford University Press, 1986)

555. Benjamin Franklin

When a religion is good, I conceive it will support itself; and when it does not support itself, and God does not take care to support it so that its professors are obliged to call for help of the civil power, 'tis a sign, I apprehend, of its being a bad one.

Anson Phelps Stokes, *Church and State in the United States* (New York: Harper, 1950), vol. I, p. 298

556. Sen. Mark Hatfield (R-Ore.)

When we allow the CIA or any other government intelligence agency to use our missionaries, we pervert the church's mission and bring discredit upon the foreign policy and credibility of the United States. For its part, the church jeopardizes the integrity of its mission when it allows itself to be used for the purposes of state.

Remarks, U.S. Senate, 1976

557. St. Hilary of Poitiers, Fourth-Century Church Father

The utter folly of our time is lamentable, that men should think to assist God with human help and to protect the Church of Christ by worldly ambition.

Quoted in M. Searle Bates, *Religious Liberty: An Inquiry* (New York: International Missionary Council, 1945), p. 138

558. President James Madison

Religion flourishes in greater purity without than with the aid of government.

Letter to Edward Livingston, July 10, 1822

559. Archbishop James Malone

The Catholic Church has access to a major section of the American public. Our impact on the public will be directly proportionate to the persuasiveness of our positions. We seek no special status and we should not be accorded one.

Address, Washington, D.C., November 1984

560. Justin Martyr, Second-Century Christian Apologist

Nothing is more contrary to religion than constraint.

Quoted in M. Searle Bates, *Religious Liberty: An Inquiry*
(New York: International Missionary Council, 1945), p. 137

561. Leo Pfeffer

A church receiving special state favors invariably pays for them in the loss of religious freedom.

Church, State & Freedom (Boston: Beacon, 1967), p. 70

562. Rev. Lynne Posselyn

It is a basic tenet of our faith that goodness and moral action should be freely chosen and not imposed by some edict of the state.

Chairperson, Maine Council of Churches, May 1986

563. Rev. Samuel T. Spear, Episcopal Priest, Brooklyn, N.Y.

Masterly inactivity on the part of the State, in the sense of leaving the maintenance, propagation and administration of the Christian religion entirely to the voluntary principle, is just the position to call forth the intensest activity on the part of the Church. It is the best position for the State to derive from both the largest quantity of moral power which is possible to apply in this imperfect world.

Religion and the State, 1876, p. 141

564. John M. Swomley

Every church is a better church if it wins the loyalty or obedience of its people instead of relying on the government to enforce church teaching.

Church & State (November 1976)

APPENDIX 1
JUDICIAL
QUOTES

(All citations are for United States Supreme Court rulings unless otherwise indicated.)

565. *Watson* v. *Jones* (1872)

The law knows no heresy, and is committed to the support of no dogma, the establishment of no sect.

Justice Samuel Miller for the majority 13 Wallace 729

566. ⸻

The structure of our government has, for the preservation of civil liberty, rescued the temporal institutions from religious interference. On the other hand, it has secured religious liberty from the invasion of the civil authority.

Ibid. at 730

567. *Board of Education of Cincinnati* v. *Minor* (1872)

Legal Christianity is a solecism, a contradiction of terms. When Christianity asks the aid of government beyond mere impartial protection, it denies itself. Its laws are divine, and not human. Its essential interests lie beyond the reach and range of human governments. United with governments, religion never rises above the merest superstition; united with religion, government never rises above the merest despotism; and all history shows us that the more widely and completely they are separated, the better it is for both.

Judge Alfonso Taft for the Ohio Supreme Court 23 Ohio ST 211

568. *Reynolds* v. *United States* (1878)

Jefferson's use of the term "wall of separation between church and state" may be accepted almost as an authoritative declaration of the scope and effect of the amendment thus secured.

98 U.S. 145 at 164

569. *Davis* v. *Beason* (1890)

The First Amendment to the Constitution . . . was intended to allow everyone under the jurisdiction of the United States to entertain such notions respecting his relations to his maker and the duties they impose as may be approved by his judgment and conscience, and to exhibit his sentiments in such form of worship as he may think proper, not injurious to the rights of others, and to prohibit legislation for the support of any religious tenets, or the modes of worship of any sect.

Justice Stephen J. Field for the majority, 133 U.S. 333

570. *Weiss* v. *District Court* (1890)

There is no such source and cause of strife, quarrel, fights, malignant opposition, persecution, and war, and all evil in the state, as religion. Let it once enter into our civil affairs, our government would soon be destroyed.

Concurring opinion, Wisconsin Supreme Court, 76 WIS 177 44 NW 981

571. *Freeman* v. *Scheve* (1902)

The state in its function as an educator must leave the teaching of religion to the church, because the church is the only body equipped to so teach, and on it rests the responsibility. There need be no shock to the moral sense, nor to our religious instincts, in barring religious subjects from our public schools and placing them where they belong, to be properly taught.

Nebraska Supreme Court, 65 Neb. 853, 91 NW 846

572. *Ring* v. *Board of Education* (1910)

The public school is supported by the taxes which each citizen, regardless of his religion or his lack of it, is compelled to pay. The school, like the government, is simply a civil institution. It is secular and not religious in its purposes. . . . It is no part of the duty of the state to teach religion—to take the money of all and apply it to teaching the children of all the religion of a part, only. Instruction in religion must be voluntary.

Illinois Supreme Court, 245 ILL. 334, 92 NE 251

573. ———

It is precisely for the protection of the minority that constitutional limits exist. Majorities need no such protection. They can take care of themselves.

Ibid. at 254

574. ———

Christianity had its beginnings and grew under oppression. Where it has depended upon the sword of civil authority for its authority, it has been weakest.

Ibid. at 256

575. *Williams* v. *Board of Trustees* (1917)

The common school, however humble its surroundings or deficient its curriculum, is the most valuable public institution in the state, and its efficiency and worth must not be impaired or destroyed by entangling it in denominational or sectarian alliances.

Kentucky Court of Appeals, 191 S.W. 507

576. *Knowlton* v. *Baumhover* (1918)

The right of a man to worship God or even refuse to worship God, and to entertain such religious views as appeal to his individual conscience without dictation
or interference by any person or power, civil or ecclesiastical, is as fundamental
in a free government like ours as is the right to life, liberty, and the pursuit of
happiness.

Iowa Supreme Court, 182 Iowa 691, 166 NW 202, 5 A.L.R. 841

577. ———

If there is any one thing which is well settled in the policies and purposes of the
American people as a whole, it is the fixed and unalterable determination that
there shall be an absolute and unequivocal separation of church and state, and
that our public school system, supported by the taxation of the property of all
alike—Catholic, Protestant, Jew, Gentile, believer, and infidel—shall not be
used, directly or indirectly, for religious instruction, and above all, that it shall
not be made an instrumentality of proselyting influence in favor of any religious
organization, sect, creed, or belief.

Ibid.

578. *Wilkerson* v. *City of Rome* (1921)

[M]aking the reading of the King James version of the Bible a part of the worship of the public schools puts municipal approval upon the version, and thus
discriminates in favor of and aids the Protestant sects of the Christian religion.

Dissent, Georgia Supreme Court, 152 GA 652 at 774

579. *State* v. *Beal* (1930)

There are those who feel more deeply over religious matters than they do about
secular things. It would be almost unbelievable, if history did not record the
tragic fact, that men have gone to war and cut each other's throats because they
could not agree as to what was to become of them after their throats were cut.
Many sins have been committed in the name of religion. Alas! The spirit of pro-
scription is never kind. It is the unhappy quality of religious disputes that they

are always bitter. For some reason, too deep to fathom, men contend more furiously over the road to heaven, which they cannot see, than over their visible walks on earth. . . .

Chief Justice Walter P. Stacy for the North Carolina Supreme Court 199 NC 278, 302

580. *Hamilton* v. *Regents of the University of California* (1934)

I assume for present purposes that the religious liberty protected by the First Amendment against invasion by the nation is protected by the Fourteenth Amendment against invasion by the states.

Justice Benjamin N. Cardozo, concurring opinion, 293 U.S. 245

581. *Traub et al.* v. *Brown* (1934)

We are of the opinion that to furnish free transportation to pupils attending sectarian schools, is to aid the schools. It helps build up, strengthen and make successful the schools as organizations.

Delaware Supreme Court, 172 Atl. 835 at 837

582. *Judd et al.* v. *Board of Education* (1938)

While a close compact has existed between the Church and State in other governments, the Federal government and each State government from their respective beginnings have followed the new concept whereby the State deprived itself of all control over religion and has refused sectaries any participation in or jurisdiction or control over the civil prerogatives of the State. And so in all civil affairs there has been a complete separation of Church and State jealously guarded and unflinchingly maintained. In conformity with that concept, education in State supported schools must be non-partisan and nonsectarian. This involves no discrimination between individuals or classes. It invades the religious rights of no one.

New York Supreme Court, 15 N.E. (2d) 576 at 581, 582

583. *Cantwell* v. *Connecticut* (1940)

The First Amendment declares that Congress shall make no law respecting an establishment of religion or prohibiting the free exercise thereof. The Fourteenth Amendment has rendered the legislatures of the states as incompetent as Congress to enact such laws. The constitutional inhibition of legislation on the subject of religion has a double aspect. On the one hand, it forestalls compulsion by law of the acceptance of any creed or the practice of any form of worship. Freedom of conscience and freedom to adhere to such religious organizations or form of worship as the individual may choose cannot be restricted by law. On the other hand, it safeguards the free exercise of the chosen form of religion.

Justice Owen J. Roberts for the majority, 310 U.S. 303

584. *West Virginia State Board of Education* v. *Barnette* (1943)

The very purpose of a Bill of Rights was to withdraw certain subjects from the vicissitudes of political controversy, to place them beyond the reach of majorities and officials and to establish them as legal principles to be applied by the courts. One's right to freedom of worship and other fundamental rights may not be submitted to vote; they depend on the outcome of no elections.

Justice Robert H. Jackson for the majority, 319 U.S. 638

585. ———

If there is any fixed star in our constitutional constellation, it is that no official, high or petty, can prescribe what shall be orthodox in politics, nationalism, religion, or other matters of opinion or force citizens to confess by word or act their faith therein.

Ibid. at 642

586. ———

The great leaders of the American Revolution were determined to remove political support from every religious establishment. . . . So far as the state was concerned, there was to be neither orthodoxy nor heterodoxy. And so Jefferson and those who followed him wrote guarantees of religious freedom into our constitutions. Religious minorities as well as religious majorities were to be equal in the eyes of the political state.

Justice Felix Frankfurter, dissent, 319 U.S. 653

587. ———

The essence of the religious freedom guaranteed by our Constitution is therefore this: no religion shall either receive the state's support or incur its hostility. Religion is outside the sphere of political government. . . . An act compelling profession of allegiance to a religion, no matter how subtly or tenuously promoted, is bad.

Ibid. at 654

588. *United States* v. *Ballard* (1944)

Heresy trials are foreign to our Constitution. Men may believe what they cannot prove. They may not be put to the proof of their religious doctrine or beliefs. Religious experiences which are as real as life to some may be incomprehensible to others.

Justice William O. Douglas for the majority, 322 U.S. 86

589. ———

The First Amendment does not select any one group or any one type of religion for preferred treatment.

Ibid. at 87

590. ———

The Fathers of the Constitution were not unaware of the varied and extreme views of religious sects, of the violence of disagreement among them, and of the lack of any one religious creed on which all men would agree. They fashioned a charter of government which envisaged the widest possible toleration of conflicting views. Man's relation to his God was made no concern of the state. He was granted the right to worship as he pleased and to answer to no man for the verity of his religious views.

Ibid. at 87

591. *Prince* v. *Massachusetts* (1944)

No chapter in human history has been so largely written in terms of persecution and intolerance as the one dealing with religious freedom. From ancient times to the present day, the ingenuity of man has known no limits in its ability to forge weapons of oppression for use against those who dare to express or practice unorthodox religious beliefs.

Justice Frank Murphy, dissent, 321 U.S. 176

592. ———

Religious freedom is too sacred a right to be restricted or prohibited in any degree without convincing proof that a legitimate interest of the state is in grave danger.

Ibid.

593. ———

Parents may be free to become martyrs themselves. But it does not follow they are free, in identical circumstances, to make martyrs of their children before they have reached the age of full and legal discretion when they can make that choice for themselves.

Justice Wiley Rutledge, dissent, 321 U.S. 170

594. *Everson* v. *Board of Education* (1947)

The "establishment of religion" clause of the First Amendment means at least this: Neither a state nor the Federal Government can set up a church. Neither can pass laws which aid one religion, aid all religions, or prefer one religion over another. Neither can force nor influence a person to go to or to remain away from church against his will or force him to profess a belief or disbelief in any religion. No person can be punished for entertaining or professing religious beliefs or disbeliefs, for church attendance or non-attendance. No tax in any amount, large or small, can be levied to support any religious activities or institutions, whatever they may be called, or whatever form they may adopt to teach or practice religion. Neither a state nor the Federal Government can, openly or secretly, participate in the affairs of any religious organizations or groups and vice versa. In the words of Jefferson, the clause against establishment of religion by law was intended to erect "a wall of separation between church and state."

Justice Hugo L. Black for the majority, 330 U.S. 15, 16

595. ———

The First Amendment has erected a wall between church and state. That wall must be kept high and impregnable. We could not approve the slightest breach.

Ibid. at 18

596. ———

The [First] Amendment's purpose was not to strike merely at the official establishment of a single sect, creed, or religion, outlawing only a formal relation such as had prevailed in England and some of the colonies. Necessarily it was to uproot all such relationships. But the object was broader than separating church and state in this narrow sense. It was to create a complete and permanent separation of the spheres of religious activity and civil authority by comprehensively forbidding every form of public aid or support for religion.

Justice Wiley Rutledge, dissent, ibid. at 31, 32

597. ———

Public money devoted to payment of religious cost, educational or other, brings the quest for more. It brings, too, the struggle of sect against sect for the larger share or for any. . . . That is precisely the history of societies which have had an established religion and dissident groups. It is the very thing Jefferson and Madison experienced and sought to guard against, whether in its blunt or in its more screened forms. The end of such strife cannot be other than to destroy the cherished liberty. . . .

Ibid. at 53, 54

598. ———

It is not because religious teaching does not promote the public or the individual's welfare, but because neither is furthered when the state promotes religious education, that the Constitution forbids it to do so.

Ibid. at 52

599. ———

We have staked the very existence of our country on the faith that a complete separation between the state and religion is best for the state and best for religion.

Ibid. at 59

600. ———

The Constitution requires, not comprehensive identification of state with religion, but complete separation.

Ibid. at 60

601. *McCollum v. Board of Education* (1948)

The First Amendment rests upon the premise that both religion and government can best work to achieve their lofty aims if each is left free from the other within its respective sphere.

Justice Hugo Black for the majority, 333 U.S. 212

602. ———

The secular public school did not imply indifference to the basic role of religion in the life of the people, nor rejection of religious education as a means of fostering it. . . . The non-sectarian or secular public school was the means of reconciling freedom in general with religious freedom.

Justice Felix Frankfurter, concurring opinion, ibid. at 216

603. ———

[L]ong before the Fourteenth Amendment subjected the states to new limitations, the prohibition of furtherance by the state of religious instruction became the guiding principle, in law and feeling, of the American people.

Ibid. at 215

604. ———

Zealous watchfulness against fusion of secular and religious activities by government itself, through any of its instruments, but especially through its educational agencies, was the democratic response of the American community to the particular needs of a young and growing nation, unique in the composition of its people.

Ibid. at 215

605. ———

Separation means separation, not something less. Jefferson's metaphor in describing the relation between Church and State speaks of a "wall of separation," not a fine line easily overstepped.

Ibid. at 231

606. ———

The public school is at once the symbol of our democracy and the most pervasive means for promoting our common destiny. In no activity of the state is it more vital to keep out divisive forces than in its schools, to avoid confusing, not to say fusing, what the Constitution sought to keep strictly apart.

Ibid.

607. ———

The modern public school derived from a philosophy of freedom reflected in the First Amendment.

Ibid. at 214

608. *Burstyn* v. *Wilson* (1952)

It is not the business of government in our nation to suppress real or imagined attacks upon a particular religious doctrine, whether they appear in publications, speeches, or motion pictures.

Majority opinion, 343 U.S. 495

609. *Kedroff* v. *St. Nicholas Cathedral* (1952)

Ours is a government which by the law of its being allows no statute, state or national, that prohibits the free exercise of religion.

Justice Stanley Reed for the majority, 344 U.S. 120

610. *Zorach* v. *Clauson* (1952)

It is precisely because eighteenth century Americans were a religious people divided into many fighting sects that we were given the constitutional mandate to keep church and state completely separate. . . .

Justice Hugo L. Black, dissent, 343 U.S. 318, 319

611. ———

State help to religion injects political and party prejudices into a holy field. It too often substitutes force for prayer, hate for love, and persecution for persuasion. Government should not be allowed, under cover of the soft euphemism of "co-operation," to steal into the sacred area of religious choice.

Ibid. at 320

612. ———

The day that this country ceases to be free for irreligion it will cease to be free for religion—except for the sect that can win political power. . . . We start down a rough road when we begin to mix compulsory public education with compulsory godliness.

Justice Robert H. Jackson, dissent, Ibid. at 325

613. *Tudor v. Board of Education of Rutherford* (1953)

[T]o permit the distribution of the King James version of the Bible in the public schools of this state would be to cast aside all the progress made in the United States and throughout New Jersey in the field of religious toleration and freedom. We would be renewing the ancient struggles among the various religious faiths to the detriment of all. This we must decline to do.

Supreme Court of New Jersey, 14 NJ 31

614. *McGowan v. Maryland* (1961)

[T]hose who fashioned the First Amendment decided that if and when God is to be served, His service will not be motivated by coercive measures of government. "Congress shall make no law respecting an establishment of religion, or prohibiting the free exercise thereof"—such is the command of the First Amendment made applicable to the State by reason of the Due Process Clause of the Fourteenth. This means, as I understand it, that if a religious leaven is to be worked into the affairs of our people, it is to be done by individuals and groups, not by the Government. This necessarily means, first, that the dogma, creed, scruples, or practices of no religious group or sect are to be preferred over those of any others; second, that no one shall be interfered with by government for practicing the religion of his choice; third, that the State cannot compel one so to conduct himself as not to offend the religious scruples of another. The idea, as I understand it, was to limit the power of government to act in religious matters, not to limit the freedom of religious men to act religiously nor to restrict the freedom of atheists or agnostics.

The First Amendment commands government to have no interest in theology or ritual; it admonishes government to be interested in allowing religious freedom to flourish—whether the result is to produce Catholics, Jews, or Protestants, or to turn the people toward the path of Buddha, or to end in a predominantly Moslem nation, or to produce in the long run atheists or agnostics. On matters of this kind government must be neutral. This freedom plainly includes freedom from religion with the right to believe, speak, write, publish, and advocate antireligious programs. Certainly the "free exercise" clause does not require that everyone embrace the theology of some church or of some faith, or observe the religious practices of any majority or minority sect. The First Amendment by its "establishment" clause prevents, of course, the selection by government of an "official" church. Yet the ban plainly extends farther than that. We said in *Everson v. Board of Education* that it would be an "establishment" of a religion if the government financed one church or several churches. For what better way to "establish" an institution than to find the fund that will support it? The "establishment" clause protects citizens also against any law which selects any religious custom, practice, or ritual, puts the force of government behind it, and fines, imprisons, or otherwise penalizes a person for not observing it. The Government plainly could not join forces with one religious group and decree a universal and symbolic circumcision. Nor could it require all children to be baptized or give tax exemptions only to those whose children were baptized.

Justice William O. Douglas, dissent, 366 U.S. 563, 564

615. *Torcaso* v. *Watkins* (1961)

We repeat and again reaffirm that neither a state nor the federal government can constitutionally force a person "to profess a belief or disbelief in any religion." Neither can constitutionally pass laws or impose requirements which aid all religions as against non-believers, and neither can aid those religions based on a belief in the existence of God as against those religions founded on different beliefs.

Justice Hugo L. Black, for the majority, 367 U.S. 495

616. *Engel* v. *Vitale* (1962)

It is no part of the business of government to compose official prayers for any group of the American people to recite as part of a religious program carried on by government.

Justice Hugo L. Black, for the majority, 370 U.S. 425

617. ———

It is neither sacrilegious nor antireligious to say that each separate government in this country should stay out of the business of writing or sanctioning official prayers and leave that purely religious function to the people themselves and to those the people choose to look to for religious guidance.

Ibid. at 435

618. ———

It is a matter of history that this very practice of establishing governmentally composed prayers for religious services was one of the reasons which caused many of our early colonists to leave England and seek religious freedom in America. . . .

Ibid. at 425

619. ———

By the time of the adoption of the Constitution, our history shows that there was a widespread awareness among many Americans of the dangers of a union of Church and State. These people knew, some of them from bitter personal experience, that one of the greatest dangers to the freedom of the individual to worship in his own way lay in the Government's placing its official stamp of approval upon one particular kind of prayer or one particular form of religious services. They knew the anguish, hardship, and bitter strife that could come when zealous religious groups struggled with one another to obtain the Government's stamp of approval from each King, Queen, or Protector that came to temporary power. The Constitution was intended to avert a part of this danger by leaving the government of this country in the hands of the people rather than in the hands of any monarch. But this safeguard was not enough. Our Founders were no more willing to let the content of their prayers and their privilege of praying whenever they pleased be influenced by the ballot box than they were to let these vital matters of personal conscience depend upon the succession of monarchs. The First Amendment was added to the Constitution to stand as a guarantee that neither the power nor the prestige of the Federal Government would be used to control, support, or influence the kinds of prayer the American people can say—that the people's religions must not be subjected to the pressures of government for change each time a new political administration is elected to office. Under that Amendment's prohibition against governmental establishment of religion, as reinforced by the provisions of the Fourteenth Amendment, government in this country, be it state or federal, is without power to prescribe by law any particular form of prayer which is to be used as an official prayer in carrying on any program of governmentally sponsored religious activity.

Ibid. at 429, 430

620. ———

When the power, prestige and financial support of government is placed behind a particular religious belief, the indirect coercive pressure upon religious minorities to conform to the prevailing officially approved religion is plain. . . . The same history showed that many people lost their respect for any religion that had relied upon the support of government to spread its faith.

Ibid. at 431

621. *Abington School District* v. *Schempp* (1963)

The place of religion in our society is an exalted one, achieved through a long tradition of reliance on the home, the church, and the inviolable citadel of the individual heart and mind. We have come to recognize through bitter experience that it is not within the power of government to invade that citadel, whether its purpose or effect be to aid or oppose, to advance or retard. In the relationship between man and religion, the State is firmly committed to a position of neutrality.

Justice Tom Clark, for the majority, 374 U.S. 226

622. ———

The public schools are supported entirely, in most communities, by public funds— funds exacted not only from parents, nor alone from those who hold particular religious views, nor indeed from those who subscribe to any creed at all. It is implicit in the history and character of American public education that the public schools serve a uniquely public function: the training of American citizens in an atmosphere free of parochial, divisive, or separatist influence of any sort—an atmosphere in which children may assimilate a heritage common to all American groups and religions. This is a heritage neither theistic nor atheistic, but simply civic and patriotic.

Justice William J. Brennan, concurring opinion, 374 U.S. 241, 242

623. ———

The State must be steadfastly neutral in all matters of faith, and neither favor nor inhibit religion. . . . Government cannot sponsor religious exercises in the public schools without jeopardizing that neutrality.

Ibid. at 299

624. ———

Any version of the Bible is inherently sectarian. . . . The sectarian character of
the Holy Bible has been at the core of the whole controversy over religious practices in the public schools throughout its long and often bitter history.

Ibid. at 282, 283

625. ———

The principles which we reaffirm and apply today can hardly be thought novel
or radical. They are, in truth, as old as the Republic itself, and have always been
as integral a part of the First Amendment as the very words of that charter of
religious liberty.

Ibid. at 304

626. ———

What the Framers meant to foreclose, and what our decisions under the Establishment Clause have forbidden, are those involvements of religious with secular institutions which (a) serve the essentially religious activities of religious
institutions; (b) employ the organs of government for essentially religious purposes; or (c) use essentially religious means to serve governmental ends, where
secular means would suffice. When the secular and religious institutions become
involved in such a manner, there inhere in the relationship precisely whose dangers—as much to church as to state—which the Framers feared would subvert
religious liberty and the strength of a system of secular government.

Ibid. at 294, 295

627. ———

The most effective way to establish any institution is to finance it, and this truth
is reflected in the appeals by church groups for public funds to finance their religious schools.

Justice William O. Douglas, concurring opinion, ibid. at 229

628. ———

What may not be done directly may not be done indirectly, lest the Establishment Clause become a mockery.

Ibid. at 230

629. *Sherbert* v. *Verner* (1963)

The door of the Free Exercise Clause stands tightly closed against any governmental regulation of religious beliefs as such. Government may neither compel affirmation of a repugnant belief, nor penalize or discriminate against individuals or groups because they hold religious views abhorrent to the authorities; nor employ the taxing power to inhibit the dissemination of particular religious views.

Justice William J. Brennan, for the majority, 374 U.S. 402

630. ———

I am convinced that no liberty is more essential to the continued vitality of the free society which our Constitution guarantees than is the religious liberty protected by the Free Exercise Clause explicit in the First Amendment and imbedded in the Fourteenth.

Justice Potter Stewart, concurring opinion, 374 U.S. 413

631. *Board of Education* v. *Allen* (1968)

The First Amendment's prohibition against governmental establishment of religion was written on the assumption that state aid to religion and religious schools generates discord, disharmony, hatred, and strife among our people, and that any government that supplies such aids is to that extent a tyranny.

Justice John Marshall Harlan, concurring opinion, 392 U.S. 254

632. ———

Now that "secular" textbooks will pour into religious schools, we can rest assured that a contest will be on to provide those books for religious schools which the dominant religious group concludes best reflect the theocentric or other philosophy of the particular church.

Justice William O. Douglas, dissent, Ibid. at 265

633. *Epperson* v. *Arkansas* (1968)

There is and can be no doubt that the First Amendment does not permit the State to require that teaching and learning must be tailored to the principles or prohibitions of any religious sect or dogma.

Justice Abe Fortas, for the majority, 393 U.S. 106

634. ———

Government in our democracy, state and national, must be neutral in matters of religious theory, doctrine, and practice. It may not be hostile to any religion or to the advocacy of no-religion; and it may not aid, foster, or promote one religion or religious theory against another or even against the militant opposite. The First Amendment mandates governmental neutrality between religion and religion, and between religion and nonreligion.

Ibid. at 103, 104

635. *Flast* v. *Cohen* (1968)

Our history vividly illustrates that one of the specific evils feared by those who drafted the Establishment Clause and fought for its adoption was that the taxing and spending power would be used to favor one religion over another or to support religion in general. . . . The concern of Madison and his supporters was quite clearly that religious liberty ultimately would be the victim if government could employ its taxing and spending powers to aid one religion over another or to aid religion in general. The Establishment Clause was designed as a specific bulwark against such potential abuses of government power, and that clause of the First Amendment operates as a specific constitutional limitation upon the exercise by Congress of the taxing and spending power conferred by Art. I, Section 8.

Chief Justice Earl Warren, for the majority, 392 U.S. 103, 104

636. ———

Because that clause [the Establishment Clause] plainly prohibits taxing and spending in aid of religion, every taxpayer can claim a personal constitutional right not to be taxed for the support of a religious institution.

Justice Potter Stewart, concurring opinion, ibid. at 114

637. *Walz* v. *Tax Commission* (1970)

Churches, like newspapers also enjoying First Amendment rights, have no constitutional immunity from all taxes.

Justice William O. Douglas, dissent, 397 U.S. 707

638. ———

The religiously used real estate of the churches today constitutes a vast domain. Their assets total over $141 billion and their annual income at least $22 billion. And the extent to which they are feeding from the public trough in a variety of forms is alarming.

Ibid. at 714

639. *Lemon* v. *Kurzman* (1971)

Ordinarily political debate and division, however vigorous or even partisan, are normal and healthy manifestations of our democratic system of government, but political division along religious lines was one of the principal evils against which the First Amendment was intended to protect. The potential divisiveness of such conflict is a threat to the normal political process.

Chief Justice Warren B. Burger, for the majority, 403 U.S. 622

640. ———

Under our system the choice has been made that government is to be entirely excluded from the area of religious instruction and churches excluded from the affairs of government.

Ibid. at 625

641. ———

[W]hen a sectarian institution accepts state financial aid it becomes obligated under the Equal Protection Clause of the Fourteenth Amendment not to discriminate in admissions policies and faculty selection.

Justice William J. Brennan, concurring opinion, ibid. at 652

642. *Tilton* v. *Richardson* (1971)

The mounting wealth of the churches makes ironic their incessant demands on the public treasury.

Justice William O. Douglas, dissent, 403 U.S. 696

643. *Wright* v. *Houston Independent School District* (1972)

Teachers of science in the public schools should not be expected to avoid the discussion of every scientific issue on which some religion claims expertise.

U.S. District Court 366 F.Supp. 1208 (S.D. Texas)

644. *PEARL* v. *Nyquist* (1973)

A proper respect for both the Free Exercise and the Establishment Clauses compels the State to pursue a course of neutrality toward religion.

Justice Lewis Powell, for the majority, 413 U.S. 756 at 792

645. ———

The relevant provisions and purposes of the First Amendment, which safeguard the separation of church from state, . . . have been regarded from the beginning as among the most cherished features of our constitutional system.

Ibid. at 795

646. *Roe* v. *Wade* (1973)

The states are not free, under the guise of protecting maternal health or potential life, to intimidate women into continuing pregnancies.

Justice Harry A. Blackmun, for the majority, 410 U.S. 113

647. *Pratt* v. *Arizona Board of Regents* (1974)

We believe that the framers of the Arizona Constitution intended . . . to prohibit the use of the power and the prestige of the State or any of its agencies for
the support or favor of one religion over another, or of religion over nonreligion.
The State is mandated by this constitutional provision to be absolutely impartial when it comes to the question of religious preference, and public money or
property may not be used to promote or favor any particular religious sect or
denomination or religion generally.

520 P.2d 514 (Arizona Supreme Court)

648. *Roemer* v. *Board of Public Works* (1976)

The discrete interests of government and religion are mutually best served when
each avoids too close a proximity to the other.

Justice William J. Brennan, for the majority, 426 U.S. 772

649. *Fox* v. *City of Los Angeles* (1978)

The state must be neutral as between those persons with religious beliefs and
those without religious beliefs.

587 P.2d 663 (California Supreme Court)

650. *Thomas* v. *Review Board* (1981)

Where the state conditions receipt of an important benefit upon conduct pro-
scribed by a religious faith, or whether it denied such a benefit because of conduct mandated by religious belief, thereby putting substantial pressure on an
adherent to modify his behavior and to violate his beliefs, a burden upon religion exists. While the compulsion may be indirect, the infringement upon free
exercise is nonetheless substantial.

Chief Justice Warren E. Burger, for the majority, 450 U.S. 718

651. *Beck* v. *McElrath* (1982)

Bringing their convictions to bear, the framers of our Constitution were determined that every individual must be free to exercise or not to practice religious

beliefs in accordance with the dictates of his conscience, and that government must stay out of religious affairs entirely.

Judge L. Clure Morton for the U.S. District Court 584 F.Supp. 1161

652. *Larkin* v. *Grendel's Den* (1982)

[T]he core rationale underlying the Establishment Clause is preventing "a fusion of governmental and religious functions." *Abingdon School District* v. *Schempp*. The Framers did not set up a system of government in which important, discretionary governmental powers would be delegated to or shared with religious institutions.

Chief Justice Warren E. Burger, for the majority, 459 U.S. 127

653. *Larson* v. *Valente* (1982)

The clearest command of the Establishment Clause is that one religious denomination cannot be officially preferred over another.

Justice William J. Brennan, for the majority, 456 U.S. 244

654. *McLean* v. *Arkansas Board of Education* (1982)

The application and content of First Amendment principles are not determined by public opinion polls or by a majority vote. Whether the proponents of Act 590 constitute the majority or the minority is quite irrelevant under a constitutional system of government. No group, no matter how large or small, may use the organs of government, of which the public schools are the most conspicuous and influential, to foist its religious beliefs on others.

District Judge William R. Overton, 579 F.Supp. 1255 (E.D. Ark.)

655. *Valley Forge College* v. *Americans United* (1982)

Each, and indeed every, federal taxpayer suffers precisely the injury that the Establishment Clause guards against when the Federal Government directs that funds be taken from the pocketbooks of the citizenry and placed into the coffers of the ministry.

Justice William J. Brennan, dissent, 454 U.S. 509

656. *Mueller* v. *Allen* (1983)

The Establishment Clause of the First Amendment prohibits a State from subsidizing religious education, whether it does so directly or indirectly.

Thurgood Marshall, dissent, 463 U.S. 388 at 404

657. *Lynch* v. *Donnelly* (1984)

The Establishment Clause prohibits government from making adherence to a
religion relevant in any way to a person's standing in the political community.

Justice Sandra Day O'Connor, concurring opinion, 465 U.S. 668 at 687

658. ———

What is crucial is that a government practice not have the effect of communi-
cating a message of government endorsement or disapproval of religion.

Ibid.

659. ———

The import of the Court's decision is to encourage use of the creche in a munic-
ipally sponsored display, a setting where Christians feel constrained in acknowledging its symbolic meaning and non-Christians feel alienated by its presence.
Surely, this is a misuse of a sacred symbol.

Justice Harry B. Blackmun, dissent, ibid. at 727

660. ———

The prestige of the government has been conferred on the beliefs associated
with the creche. The effect on minority religious groups, as well as those who
may reject all religion, is to convey the message that their views are not similarly
worthy of public recognition nor entitled to public support. It was precisely this
sort of religious chauvinism that the Establishment Clause was intended forever
to prohibit.

Justice William J. Brennan, dissent, ibid. at 701

661. *School District of Grand Rapids* v. *Ball* (1985)

Although Establishment Clause jurisprudence is characterized by few absolutes, the Clause does absolutely prohibit government-financed or government-sponsored indoctrination into the beliefs of a particular religious faith. Such indoctrination, if permitted to occur, would have devastating effects on the right of each individual voluntarily to determine what to believe (and what not to believe) free of any coercive pressures from the state. . . .

Justice William C. Brennan, for the majority, 473 U.S. 373 at 385

662. ———

Providing for the education of schoolchildren is surely a praiseworthy purpose. But our cases have consistently recognized that even such a praiseworthy, secular purpose cannot validate government aid to parochial schools when the aid has the effect of promoting a single religion or religion generally or when the aid unduly entangles the government in matters religious. For just as religion throughout history has provided spiritual comfort, guidance, and inspiration to many, it can also serve powerfully to divide societies and to exclude those whose beliefs are not in accord with particular religions or sects that have from time to time achieved dominance. The solution to this problem adopted by the Framers and consistently recognized by this Court is jealously to guard the right of every individual to worship according to the dictates of conscience while requiring the government to maintain a course of neutrality among religions, and between religion and nonreligion.

Ibid.

663. ———

Our cases have recognized that the Establishment Clause guards against more than direct, state-funded efforts to indoctrinate youngsters in specific religious beliefs. Government promotes religion as effectively when it fosters a close identification of its powers and responsibilities with those of any—or all—religious denominations as when it attempts to inculcate specific religious doctrines. If this identification conveys a message of government endorsement or disapproval of religion, a core purpose of the Establishment Clause is violated.

Ibid. at 389

664. *Wallace* v. *Jaffree* (1985)

The government must pursue a course of complete neutrality toward religion.

Justice John Paul Stevens, for the majority, 472 U.S. 38

665. ———

When the underlying principle has been examined in the crucible of litigation, the court has unambiguously concluded that the individual freedom of conscience protected by the First Amendment embraces the right to select any religious faith or none at all.

Ibid. at 52, 53

666. *ACLU* v. *City of Birmingham* (1986)

It is difficult to believe that the city's practice of displaying an unadorned creche on the City Hall lawn would not convey to a non-Christian a message that the city endorses Christianity.

U.S. Court of Appeals for the Sixth Circuit, 797 F.2d 1561

667. ———

Since the majority does not need its protections, the Bill of Rights was adopted for the benefit and protection of minorities.

Ibid.

668. *Goldman* v. *Weinberger* (1986)

Through our Bill of Rights, we pledged ourselves to attain a level of human freedom and dignity that had no parallel in history. Our constitutional commitment to religious freedom and acceptance of religious pluralism is one of our greatest achievements in that noble endeavor. Almost two hundred years after the First Amendment was drafted, tolerance and respect for all religions still set us apart from most other countries and draws to our shores refugees from religious persecution from around the world.

Justice William Brennan, dissent, 475 U.S. 503

669. *Hardwick* v. *Bowers* (1986)

A state can no more punish private behavior because of religious intolerance than it can punish such behavior because of racial animus.

Justice Harry Blackmun, dissent, 478 U.S. 186

670. *Mainger* v. *Mukilteo School District* (1986)

The Supreme Court has continually been zealous in protecting the right of school children to be free from sectarian influence by school authorities. Thus, practices which may be acceptable for an adult audience or a public forum may be unacceptable for public schools where attendance is mandatory and the desire to conform is typical among youth of such age.

Judge Dennis Brett. No. 85-2-0467102
(Superior Court for the County of Snohomish, Washington)

671. *Ohio Civil Rights Commission* v. *Dayton Christian Schools* (1986)

Even religious schools cannot claim to be wholly free from state regulation.

Chief Justice William Rehnquist, for the majority, 476 U.S. 1103

672. *American Jewish Congress* v. *City of Chicago* (1987)

A crèche in City hall brings together church and state in a manner that unmistakably suggests their alliance. The display in this case advanced religion by sending a message to the people of Chicago that the city approved of Christianity.

U.S. Circuit Court of Appeals for the Seventh Circuit, 827 F.2d 120

673. *Cooper* v. *Eugene School District* (1987)

Recognition that freedom of religion for all implies official sponsorship of none has grown with the growing diversity of the nation itself.

Justice Hans Linde, Oregon Supreme Court

674. *Hobbie* v. *Unemployment Appeals Board* (1987)

The First Amendment protects the free exercise rights of employees who adopt religious beliefs or convert from one faith to another after they are hired.

Justice William J. Brennan, for the majority, 480 U.S. 136

675. *Edwards* v. *Aguillard* (1987)

The Louisiana Creationism Act advances a religious doctrine by requiring either the banishment of the theory of evolution from public school classrooms or the presentation of a religious viewpoint that rejects evolution in its entirety. The Act violates the Establishment Clause of the First Amendment because it seeks to employ the symbolic and financial support of government to achieve a religious purpose.

Justice William J. Brennan, for the majority, 107 S.Ct. 2573

676. ———

In sum, I find that the language and the legislative history of the Balanced Treatment Act unquestionably demonstrate that its purpose is to advance a particular religious belief. Although the discretion of state and local authorities over public school curricula is broad, "the First Amendment does not permit the State to require that teaching and learning must be tailored to the principles or prohibitions of any religious sect or dogma."

Justice Lewis Powell, concurring opinion, ibid.

677. *Bowen* v. *Kendrick* (1988)

The risk of advancing religion at public expense, and of creating an appearance that the government is endorsing the medium and the message, is much greater when the religious organization is directly engaged in pedagogy, with the express intent of shaping belief and changing behavior, than where it is neutrally dispensing medication, food, or shelter.

Justice Harry Blackmun, dissent, 487 U.S. 589 at 641

678. *Hewitt* v. *Joyner* (1991)

The state may not discriminate between religions or prefer one religion over another.

U.S. Court of Appeals for the Ninth Circuit, 940 F2d. 1561, at 1563

679. *Lee* v. *Weisman* (1992)

No holding by this Court suggests that a school can persuade or compel a student to participate in a religious exercise.

Justice Anthony Kennedy, for the majority, 505 U.S. 577 at 599

680. ———

Government pressure to participate in a religious activity is an obvious indication that the government is endorsing or promoting religion. But it is not enough that the government refrain from compelling religious practices: It must not engage in them either.

Ibid. at 604

681. ———

[T]he Establishment Clause forbids state-sponsored prayers in public school settings no matter how nondenominational the prayers may be. In barring the State from sponsoring generically theistic prayers where it could not sponsor sectarian ones, we hold true to a line of precedent from which there is no adequate historical case to depart.

Justice David Souter, concurring opinion, 505 U.S. 577 at 610

682. ———

[H]istory neither contradicts nor warrants reconsideration of the settled principle that the Establishment Clause forbids support for religion in general no less than support for one religion or some.

David Souter, concurring opinion, 505 U.S. 577 at 616

683. ———

The state may not favor or endorse either religion generally over non-religion or one religion over others. This principle against favoritism and endorsement has become the foundation of Establishment Clause jurisprudence, ensuring that religious belief is irrelevant to every citizen's standing in the political community.

Ibid. at 627

684. ———

[T]he government's sponsorship of prayer at the graduation ceremony is most reasonably understood as an official endorsement of religion.

Ibid. at 630

685. ———

When public school officials, armed with the state's authority, convey an endorsement of religion to their students, they strike near the core of the Establishment Clause. However ceremonial their messages may be, they are flatly unconstitutional.

Ibid. at 631

686. *Kiryas Joel* v. *Grumet* (1994)

A religious accommodation demands careful scrutiny to ensure that it does not so burden nonadherents or discriminate against either religions as to become an establishment.

Justice Anthony Kennedy, concurring opinion, 114 S.Ct. 2481 at 2501

687. ———

People who share a common religious belief or lifestyle may live together without sacrificing the basic rights of self-governance that all American citizens enjoy, so long as they do not use those rights to establish their religious faith. Religion flourishes in community, and the Establishment Clause must not be construed as some sort of homogenizing solvent that forces unconventional religious groups to choose between assimilating to mainstream American culture or losing their political rights. There is more than a fine line, however, between the voluntary association that leads to a political community comprised of people who share a common religious faith, and the forced separation that occurs when the government draws explicit political boundaries on the basis of peoples' faith.

Ibid. at 2505

688. *Rosenberger* v. *University of Virginia* (1995)

Using public funds for the direct subsidization of preaching the word is categorically forbidden under the Establishment Clause, and if the Clause was meant to accomplish nothing else, it was meant to bar this use of public money. Evidence on this subject antedates even the Bill of Rights itself, as may be seen in the writings of Madison, whose authority on questions about the meaning of the Establishment Clause is well settled.

Justice David Souter, dissent, 115 S.Ct. 2510 at 2535

689. *Capitol Square* v. *Pinette* (1995)

The Establishment Clause should be construed to create a strong presumption against the installation of unattended religious symbols on public property.

Justice John Paul Stevens, dissent, 115 S.Ct. 2440 at 2464

690. ———

The Establishment Clause does not merely prohibit the State from favoring one religious sect over others. It also proscribes state action supporting the establishment of a number of religions, as well as the official endorsement of religion in preference to nonreligion.

Ibid. at 2470

691. *ACLU* v. *Black Horse Pike*
Regional Board of Education (1996)

The First Amendment does not allow the state to erect a policy that only respects religious views that are popular because the largest majority can not be licensed to impose its religious preferences upon the smallest minority.

U.S. Court of Appeals for the Third Circuit, May 24, 1996

692. *Herdahl* v. *Pontotoc County School District* (1996)

The Bill of Rights was created to protect the minority from tyranny by the majority. . . . To say that the majority should prevail simply because of the numbers is to forget the purpose of the Bill of Rights.

887 F.Supp. 902 (N.D. Miss.)

693. ─────

The court is firmly persuaded that the predominant purpose of the Bible class is not secular, rather, it is the part of a concerted effort by the religious sponsors of the class, fully condoned by the District, to inculcate students with the beliefs and moral code of fundamentalist Christianity—an admirable goal perhaps for some private citizens or for a private religious school, but a forbidden one for the government.

Ibid.

694. ─────

These practices obviously violate the neutrality that a public teacher is required to maintain toward religion, and constitute impermissible religious instruction and endorsement of religion by a public official which crosses the wall the constitution erected between the scepter and the cross.

Ibid.

695. *Agostini* v. *Felton* (1997)

The State is forbidden to subsidize religion directly and is just as surely forbidden to act in any way that could reasonably be viewed as religious endorsement.

Justice David Souter, dissent, 521 U.S. 203 at 242

696. ─────

The flat ban on subsidization antedates the Bill of Rights and has been an unwavering rule in Establishment Clause cases.

Ibid. at 243

697. *City of Boerne* v. *Flores* (1997)

The Religion Clauses of the Constitution represent a profound commitment to religious liberty. Our nation's founders conceived of a Republic receptive to voluntary religious expression, not of a secular society in which religious expression is tolerated only when it does not conflict with a generally applicable law.

Justice Sandra Day O'Connor, dissent, 521 U.S. 507 at 564

698. *Mitchell* v. *Helms* (2000)

The establishment prohibition of government religious funding serves more than one end. It is meant to guarantee the right of individual conscience against compulsion, to protect the integrity of religion against the corrosion of secular support, and to preserve the unity of political society against the implied exclusion of the less favored and the antagonism of controversy over public support for religious causes.

Justice David Souter, dissent

699. *Gentala* v. *City of Tucson* (2000)

Taxpayer funds may not be used to support a religious organization.

Judge Harry Pregerson, dissent, U.S. Court of Appeals for the Ninth Circuit, Case Number 97-17062 decided April 20, 2000

700. ———

The use of taxpayer money to pay a religious organization's bills is a blatant example of an Establishment Clause violation.

Ibid.

701. *Simmons-Harris* v. *Zelman* (2000)

To approve this program would approve the actual diversion of government aid to religious institutions in endorsement of religious education, something "in tension" with the precedents of the Supreme Court. We find that when, as here, the government has established a program which does not permit private citizens to direct government aid freely as in their private choice, but which restricts their choice to a panoply of religious institutions and spaces with only a few alternative possibilities, then the Establishment Clause is violated. This scheme involves the grant of state aid directly and predominantly to the coffers of the private religious schools, and it is unquestioned that these institutions incorporate religious concepts, motives, and themes into all facets of their educational planning. There is no neutral aid when that aid primarily flows to religious institutions; nor is there truly "private choice" when the available choices resulting from the program design are predominantly religious.

U.S. Court of Appeals for the Sixth Circuit,
Case 00-3055/3060, decided December 11, 2000, FED. App. 0411P (6th Cir.)

APPENDIX 2

M JAMES ADISON

702. A Memorial and Remonstrance Against Religious Assessments

To the Honorable the General Assembly of the Commonwealth of Virginia
A Memorial and Remonstrance

We the subscribers, citizens of the said Commonwealth, having taken into serious consideration, a Bill printed by order of the last Session of General Assembly, entitled "a Bill establishing a provision for Teachers of the Christian Religion," and conceiving that the same if finally armed with the sanctions of a law, will be a dangerous abuse of power, are bound as faithful members of a free State to remonstrate against it, and to declare the reasons by which we are determined. We remonstrate against the said Bill,

1. Because we hold it for a fundamental and undeniable truth, "that Religion or the duty which we owe to our Creator and the manner of discharging it, can be directed only by reason and conviction, not by force or violence." The Religion then of every man must be left to the conviction and conscience of every man; and it is the right of every man to exercise it as these may dictate. This right is in its nature an unalienable right. It is unalienable, because the opinions of men, depending only on the evidence contemplated by their own minds cannot

follow the dictates of other men. It is unalienable also, because what is here a right towards men, is a duty towards the Creator. It is the duty of every man to render to the Creator such homage and such only as he believes to be acceptable to him. This duty is precedent, both in order of time and in degree of obligation, to the claims of Civil Society. Before any man can be considered as a member of Civil Society, he must be considered as a subject of the Governour of the Universe: And if a member of Civil Society, who enters into any subordinate Association, must always do it with a reservation of his duty to the General Authority; much more must every man who becomes a member of any particular Civil Society, do it with a saving of his allegiance to the Universal Sovereign. We maintain therefore that in matters of Religion, no man's right is abridged by the institution of Civil Society and that Religion is wholly exempt from its cognizance. True it is, that no other rule exists, by which any question which may divide a Society, can be ultimately determined, but the will of the majority; but it is also true that the majority may trespass on the rights of the minority.

2. Because if Religion be exempt from the authority of the Society at large, still less can be subject to that of the Legislative Body. The latter are but the creatures and vicegerents of the former. Their jurisdiction is both derivative and limited: it is limited with regard to the co-ordinate departments, more necessarily is it limited with regard to the constituents. The preservation of a free Government requires not merely, that the metes and bounds which separate each department of power be invariably maintained; but more especially that neither of them be suffered to overleap the great Barrier which defends the rights of the people. The Rulers who are guilty of such an encroachment, exceed the commission from which they derive their authority, and are Tyrants. The People who submit to it are governed by laws made neither by themselves nor by an authority derived from them, and are slaves.

3. Because it is proper to take alarm at the first experiment on our liberties. We hold this prudent jealousy to be the first duty of Citizens, and one of the noblest characteristics of the late Revolution. The free men of America did not wait till usurped power had strengthened itself by exercise, and entangled the question in precedents. They saw all the consequences in the principle, and they avoided the consequences by denying the principle. We revere this lesson too much soon to forget it. Who does not see that the same authority which can establish Christianity, in exclusion of all other Religions, may establish with the same ease any particular sect of Christians, in exclusion of all other Sects? that

the same authority which can force a citizen to contribute three pence only of his property for the support of any one establishment, may force him to conform to any other establishment in all cases whatsoever?

4. Because the Bill violates that equality which ought to be the basis of every law, and which is more indispensible, in proportion as the validity or expediency of any law is more liable to be impeached. If "all men are by nature equally free and independent," all men are to be considered as entering into Society on equal conditions; as relinquishing no more, and therefore retaining no less, one than another, of their natural rights. Above all are they to be considered as retaining an "*equal* title to the free exercise of Religion according to the dictates of Conscience." Whilst we assert for ourselves a freedom to embrace, to profess and to observe the Religion which we believe to be of divine origin, we cannot deny an equal freedom to those whose minds have not yet yielded to the evidence which has convinced us. If this freedom be abused, it is an offence against God, not against man. To God, therefore, not to man, must an account of it be rendered. As the Bill violates equality by subjecting some to peculiar burdens, so it violates the same principle, by granting to others peculiar exemptions. Are the Quakers and Menonists the only sects who think a compulsive support of their Religions unnecessary and unwarrantable? Can their piety alone be entrusted with the care of public worship? Ought their Religions to be endowed above all others with extraordinary privileges by which proselytes may be enticed from all others? We think too favorably of the justice and good sense of these denominations to believe that they either covet pre-eminences over their fellow citizens or that they will be seduced by them from the common opposition to the measure.

5. Because the Bill implies either that the Civil Magistrate is a competent Judge of Religious Truth; or that he may employ Religion as an engine of Civil policy. The first is an arrogant pretension falsified by the contradictory opinions of Rulers of all ages, and throughout the world; the second an unhallowed perversion of the means of salvation.

6. Because the establishment proposed by the Bill is not requisite for the support of the Christian Religion. To say that it is, is a contradiction to the Christian Religion itself, for every page of it disavows a dependence on the powers of this world; it is a contradiction to fact, for it is known that this Religion both existed and flourished, not only without the support of human laws, but in spite of every opposition from them, and not only during the period of

miraculous aid, but long after it had been left to its own evidence and the ordinary care of Providence. Nay, it is a contradiction in terms; for a Religion not invented by human policy, must have pre-existed and been supported, before it was established by human policy. It is moreover to weaken in those who profess this Religion a pious confidence in its innate excellence and the patronage of its Author; and to foster in those who still reject it, a suspicion that its friends are too conscious of its falacies to trust it to its own merits.

7. Because experience witnesseth that ecclesiastical establishments, instead of maintaining the purity and efficacy of Religion, have had a contrary operation. During almost fifteen centuries has the legal establishment of Christianity been on trial. What have been its fruits? More or less in all places, pride and indolence in the Clergy, ignorance and servility in the laity, in both, superstition, bigotry and persecution. Enquire of the Teachers of Christianity for the ages in which it appeared in its greatest lustre; those of every sect, point to the ages prior to its incorporation with Civil policy. Propose a restoration of this primitive State in which its Teachers depended on the voluntary rewards of their flocks, many of them predict its downfall. On which Side ought their testimony to have greatest weight, when for or when against their interest?

8. Because the establishment in question is not necessary for the support of the Civil Government. If it be urged as necessary for the support of Civil Government only as it is a means of supporting Religion, and it be not necessary for the latter purpose, it cannot be necessary for the former. If Religion be not within the cognizance of Civil Government how can its legal establishment be necessary to Civil Government? What influence in fact have ecclesiastical establishments had on Civil Society? In some instances they have been seen to erect a spiritual tyranny on the ruins of the Civil authority; in many instances they have been seen upholding the thrones of political tyranny; in no instance have they been seen the guardians of the liberties of the people. Rulers who wished to subvert the public liberty, may have found an established Clergy convenient auxiliaries. A just Government instituted to secure & perpetuate it needs them not. Such a Government will be best supported by protecting every Citizen in the enjoyment of his Religion with the same equal hand which protects his person and his property; by neither invading the equal rights of any Sect, nor suffering any Sect to invade those of another.

9. Because the proposed establishment is a departure from that generous policy, which, offering an Asylum to the persecuted and oppressed of every

Nation and Religion, promised a lustre to our country, and an accession to the number of its citizens. What a melancholy mark is the Bill of sudden degeneracy? Instead of holding forth an Asylum to the persecuted, it is itself a signal of persecution. It degrades from the equal rank of Citizens all those whose opinions in Religion do not bend to those of the Legislative authority. Distant as it may be in its present form from the Inquisition, it differs from it only in degree. The one is the first step, the other the last in the career of intolerance. The magnanimous sufferer under this cruel scourge in foreign Regions, must view the Bill as a Beacon on our Coast, warning him to seek some other haven, where liberty and philanthropy in their due extent may offer a more certain repose from his Troubles.

10. Because it will have a like tendency to banish our Citizens. The allurements presented by other situations are every day thinning their number. To superadd a fresh motive to emigration by revoking the liberty which they now enjoy, would be the same species of folly which has dishonoured and depopulated flourishing kingdoms.

11. Because it will destroy that moderation and harmony which the forbearance of our laws to intermeddle with Religion has produced among its several sects. Torrents of blood have been spilt in the old world, by vain attempts of the secular arm, to extinguish Religious discord, by proscribing all differences in Religious opinion. Time has at length revealed the true remedy. Every relaxation of narrow and rigorous policy, wherever it has been tried, has been found to assuage the disease. The American Theatre has exhibited proofs that equal and compleat liberty, if it does not wholly eradicate it, sufficiently destroys its malignant influence on the health and prosperity of the State. If with the salutary effects of this system under our own eyes, we begin to contract the bounds of Religious freedom, we know no name that will too severely reproach our folly. At least let warning be taken at the first fruits of the threatened innovation. The very appearance of the Bill has transformed "that Christian forbearance, love and charity," which of late mutually prevailed, into animosities and jealousies, which may not soon be appeased. What mischiefs may not be dreaded, should this enemy to the public quiet be armed with the force of a law?

12. Because the policy of the Bill is adverse to the diffusion of the light of Christianity. The first wish of those who enjoy this precious gift ought to be that it may be imparted to the whole race of mankind. Compare the number of those who have as yet received it with the number still remaining under the dominion of false

Religions; and how small is the former! Does the policy of the Bill tend to lesson the disproportion? No; it at once discourages those who are strangers to the light of revelation from coming into the Region of it; and countenances by example the nations who continue in darkness, in shutting out those who might convey it to them. Instead of Levelling as far as possible, every obstacle to the victorious progress of Truth, the Bill with an ignoble and unchristian timidity would circumscribe it with a wall of defence against the encroachments of error.

13. Because attempts to enforce by legal sanctions, acts obnoxious to so great a proportion of Citizens, tend to enervate the laws in general, and to slacken the bands of Society. If it be difficult to execute any law which is not generally deemed necessary or salutary, what must be the case, where it is deemed invalid and dangerous? And what may be the effect of so striking an example of impotency in the Government, on its general authority?

14. Because a measure of such singular magnitude and delicacy ought not to be imposed, without the clearest evidence that it is called for by a majority of citizens, and no satisfactory method is yet proposed by which the voice of the majority in this case may be determined, or its influence secured. "The people of the respective counties are indeed requested to signify their opinion respecting the adoption of the Bill to the next Session of Assembly." But the representation must be made equal, before the voice either of the Representatives or of the Counties will be that of the people. Our hope is that neither of the former will, after due consideration, espouse the dangerous principle of the Bill. Should the event disappoint us, it will still leave us in full confidence, that a fair appeal to the latter will reverse the sentence against our liberties.

15. Because finally, "the equal right of every citizen to the free exercise of his Religion according to the dictates of conscience" is held by the same tenure with all our other rights. If we recur to its origin, it is equally the gift of nature; if we weigh its importance, it cannot be less dear to us; if we consult the "Declaration of those rights which pertain to the good people of Virginia, as the basis and foundation of Government," it is enumerated with equal solemnity, or rather studied emphasis. Either then, we must say, that the Will of the Legislature is the only measure of their authority; and that in the plentitude of this authority, they may sweep away all our fundamental rights; or, that they are bound to leave this particular right untouched and sacred: Either we must say, that they may controul the freedom of the press, may abolish the Trial by jury, may swallow up the Executive and judiciary Powers of the State; nay that they

may despoil us of our very right of suffrage, and erect themselves into an independent and hereditary Assembly or, we must say, that they have no authority to enact into law the Bill under consideration. We the Subscribers say, that the General Assembly of this Commonwealth have no such authority; And that no effort may be omitted on our part against so dangerous an usurpation, we oppose to it, this remonstrance; earnestly praying, as we are in duty bound, that the Supreme Lawgiver of the Universe, by illuminating those to whom it is addressed, may on the one hand, turn their Councils from every act which would affront his holy prerogative, or violate the trust committed to them; and on the other, guide them into every measure which may be worthy of his [blessing, may re]dound to their own praise, and may establish more firmly the liberties, the prosperity and the happiness of the Commonwealth.

1785

APPENDIX 3

THOMAS JEFFERSON

703. Bill for Establishing Religious Freedom

I. Whereas Almighty God hath created the mind free; that all attempts to influence it by temporal punishments or burthens, or by civil incapacitations, tend only to beget habits of hypocrisy and meanness, and are a departure from the plan of the Holy Author of our religion, who being Lord both of body and mind, yet chose not to propagate it by coercions on either, as was in his Almighty power to do; that the impious presumption of legislators and rulers, civil as well as ecclesiastical, who being themselves but fallible and uninspired men, have assumed dominion over the faith of others, setting up their own opinions and modes of thinking as the only true and infallible, and as such endeavouring to impose them on others, hath established and maintained false religions over the greatest part of the world, and through all time; that to compel a man to furnish contributions of money for the propagation of opinions which he disbelieves, is sinful and tyrannical; that even the forcing him to support this or that teacher of his own religious persuasion, is depriving him of the comfortable liberty of giving his contributions to the particular pastor, whose morals he would make his pattern, and whose powers he feels most persuasive to righteousness, and is withdrawing from the ministry those temporary rewards, which proceeding from an approbation of their personal conduct, are an additional incitement to earnest and unremitting labours for the instruction of mankind; that our civil rights have no dependence on our religious opinions, any more than our opinions in physics or geometry; that therefore the proscribing any citizen as unworthy the public confidence by laying upon him an incapacity of being called to offices of trust and emolument, unless he profess or renounce this or that religious opinion, is depriving him injuriously of those privileges and advantages to which in common with his fellow-citizens he has a natural right; that it tends only to corrupt the principles of that religion it is meant to encourage, by bribing with a monopoly of worldly honours and emoluments, those who will externally profess and conform to it; that though indeed these are criminal who do not withstand such temptation, yet neither are those innocent who lay the bait in their way; that to suffer the civil magistrate to intrude his powers into the field of opinion, and to restrain the profession or propagation of principles on supposition of their ill tendency, is a dangerous fallacy, which at once destroys all religious liberty, because he being of course judge of that tendency will make his opinions the rule of judgment, and approve or condemn the sentiments of others only as they shall square with or differ from his own; that it is time enough for the rightful purposes of civil government, for its officers to interfere when principles break out into overt acts against peace and good order; and finally, that truth is great and will prevail if left to herself, that she is the proper and sufficient antagonist to error, and has nothing to fear from the conflict, unless by human interposition disarmed of her natural weapons, free argument and debate; errors ceasing to be dangerous when it is permitted freely to contradict them:

II. *Be it enacted by the General Assembly*, That no man shall be compelled to frequent or support any religious worship, place or ministry whatsoever, nor shall be enforced, restrained, molested, or burthened in his body or goods, nor shall otherwise suffer on account of his religious opinions or belief; but that all men shall be free to profess, and by argument to maintain, their opinions in matters of religion, and that the same shall in no wise diminish, enlarge, or affect their civil capacities.

III. And though we well know that this Assembly, elected by the people for the ordinary purposes of legislation only, have no power to restrain the acts of succeeding Assemblies, constituted with powers equal to our own, and that therefore to declare this act to be irrevocable would be of no effect in law; yet we are free to declare, and do declare, that the rights hereby asserted are of the natural rights of mankind, and that if any act shall be hereafter passed to repeal the present, or to narrow its operation, such act will be an infringement of natural right.

Approved by Virginia Legislature, 1786

APPENDIX 4

R OPPONENTS OF ELIGIOUS LIBERTY

704. *The Catholic World*

The wall of separation said to have been erected by the First Amendment exists only in the mind or rather in the imagination of legal students smoking the opium of secularism.

Editorial, April 1955

705. *Civiltá Cattólica*, Italian Jesuit Journal

In a state where the majority of people are Catholic, the church will require that legal existence be denied to error, and that if religious minorities exist, they shall have only a de facto existence without opportunity to spread their unbeliefs.

Editorial, April 1948

706. Charles Colson

Only the Church collectively can decide at what point a government becomes significantly corrupt that a believer must resist. But, with fear and trembling, I have begun to believe that however Christians in America gather to reach that consensus, we are fast approaching this point. When peaceable means and limited civil disobedience fail, . . . revolution can be justified from a Christian viewpoint.

First Things (November 1996)

707. Francis J. Connell

If the country is distinctively Catholic—that is, if the population is almost entirely Catholic, and the national life and institutions are permeated with the spirit of Catholicity—the civil rulers can consider themselves justified in restricting or preventing denominational activities hostile to the Catholic religion.

Freedom of Worship (New York: Paulist Press, 1944)

708. Rev. W. A. Criswell, Pastor, First Baptist Church, Dallas, Tex.

I believe this notion of the separation of church and state was the figment of some infidel's imagination.

Interview, *CBS Evening News*, August 23, 1984

709. ———

The election of John F. Kennedy will lead to the death of a free church and a free state.

Sermon, July 4, 1960

710. James Dobson

Nearly thirty million unborn babies have been killed since the Supreme Court issued its despicable *Roe* v. *Wade* decision in 1973. That number represents more than 10 percent of the U.S. population; and it is growing by 4,110 per day. Such bloodshed and butchery, now occurring worldwide, is unprecedented in human history, yet we've only seen the beginning. Don't tell me this crime against humanity will go unpunished! Those voiceless little people cry out to the Almighty from the incinerators and the garbage heaps where they have been discarded. Someday, this "unborn holocaust" will rain death and destruction upon our nation. Just wait. You'll see. It is in the nature of the universe. Sin inevitably devastates a people who embrace it. . . . Alas, we have chosen death! And we will have hell to put for it.

James Dobson, When God Doesn't Make Sense
(Wheaton, Ill.: Tyndale House, 1993), pp. 183–84

711. John Eidsmoe

America needs to return to the traditional, Bible-based moral standards the founding fathers believed in if our free society is to continue. If people cannot voluntarily restrain their sinful impulses through moral self-discipline, it may be necessary for the government to supply that restraint.

Christianity and the Constitution (Grand Rapids, Mich.: Baker Books, 1987), p. 382

712. Rev. Jerry Falwell

The idea that religion and politics don't mix was invented by the Devil to keep Christians from running their own country.

Sermon, July 4, 1976

713. ⸻

I hope I live to see the day when, as in the early days of our country, we won't have any public schools. The churches will have taken them over again and Christians will be running them. What a happy day that will be!

America Can Be Saved (Murfreesboro, Tenn.: Sword of the Lord, 1979), pp. 52–53

714. Pope Gregory XVI

From the most foul well of indifferentiation flows that absurd and erroneous opinion, or rather delirium, of liberty of conscience.

Encyclical, Mirari Vos, 1832

715. Rev. Mordecai Fowler Ham

If you vote for Al Smith, you're voting against Christ and you will all be damned.

Sermon, First Baptist Church, Oklahoma City, September 1928

716. Rev. R. L. Hymers, Pastor, Fundamentalist Baptist Tabernacle of Los Angeles

We will pray that God take the life of these Hitler-like men from the face of the earth.

On praying for the deaths of Justice William Brennan and four other Justices, 1986

717. Bill Keith, Louisiana State Senator

If I had my way, I would have the Book of Genesis taught in all our elementary schools.

Address, Monroe, La., 1986

718. Rev. D. James Kennedy

Today the ungodly are doing their best to destroy . . . and the club they are using to beat back the idea of religious liberty is the "wall of separation between church and state," usually in the hands of the ACLU. Like Hitler's big lie, this false doctrine has been used to brainwash the American people and to attempt to drive Christians and the Christian faith into oblivion.

D. James Kennedy with Jim Nelson Black, *Character and Destiny: A Nation in Search of Its Soul*
(Grand Rapids, Mich.: Zondervan Publishing House, 1994), p. 125

719. Ayatollah Ruhollah Khomeini

Familiarize the people with the truth of Islam so that the young generation may not think that the men of religion in the mosques of Qum and al-Najaf believe in the separation of church from state, that they study nothing other than menstruation and childbirth and that they have nothing to do with politics. The colonialists have spread in school curricula the need to separate church from the state and have deluded people into believing that the ulema [religious experts] of Islam are not qualified to interfere in the political and social affairs. The lackeys and followers of the colonialists have reiterated these words. In the prophet's time, was the church separated from the state? Were there at the time theologians and politicians? At the time of the caliphs and the time of Ali, the amir of the faithful, was the state separated from the church? Was there an agency for the church and another for the state?

The difference between the Islamic government and the constitutional governments, both monarchic and republican, lies in the fact that the people's representatives or the king's representatives are the ones who codify and legislate, whereas the power of legislation is confined to God, may He be praised, and nobody else has the right to legislate and nobody may rule by that which has not been given power by God. This is why Islam replaces the legislative council by a planning council that works to run the affairs and work of the ministries so that they may offer their services in all spheres.

Christian, Jewish, and Baha'i missionary centers are spread in Tehran to deceive people and to lead them way from the teachings and principles of religion. Isn't it a duty to destroy these centers?

Islamic Government (New York: Manor Books, 1979)

720. Rev. Tim LaHaye

I'll tell you what is wrong with America. We don't have enough of God's ministers running the country.

Address, Religious Roundtable Breakfast, *New York Times* (September 8, 1984)

721. Pope Leo XIII

All Catholics must make themselves felt as active elements in daily political life in the countries where they live. They must penetrate, wherever possible, in the administration of civil affairs; must constantly exert the utmost vigilance and energy to prevent the usages of liberty from going beyond the limits fixed by God's law. All Catholics should do all in their power to cause the constitutions of states and legislation to be modeled on the principles of the true Church.

Encyclical, *Immortale Dei*, 1885

722. Rev. Richard John Neuhaus

The separation of church and state means the separation of the law from common decency.

The Best of the Public Square, ed. J. Bottum
(New York: Institute on Religion and Public Life, 1997), p. 154

723. Pope Pius XI

It is the duty of the state to help the church maintain its religious schools by aid from public funds. . . .

Encyclical, On the Christian Education of Youth, 1929

724. President Ronald Reagan

God, the source of all knowledge, should never have been expelled from our children's classrooms.

Address, National Religious Broadcasters, Washington, D.C., January 1984

725. Rev. Marion G. (Pat) Robertson

The Supreme Court has made atheism the only acceptable religion for America's public school children.

Freedom Council fundraising letter, August 5, 1985

726. ———

The Constitution of the United States is a marvelous document for self-government by Christian people. But the minute you turn the document into the hands of non-Christian people and atheistic people they can use it to destroy the very foundation of our society. And that's what's been happening.

700 Club, December 30, 1981

727. ———

[The American public school system] steadily is attempting to do something that a few states other than the Nazis and the Soviets have attempted to do, namely, to take the children away from the parents and to educate them in a philosophy that is amoral, anti-Christian, and humanistic and to show them a collectivistic philosophy that will ultimately lead toward Marxism, socialism, and a communistic type of ideology.

700 Club, May 13, 1984

728. Rev. John A. Ryan

If there is only one true religion, and if its possession is the most important good in life for States as well as individuals, then the public profession, protection, and promotion of this religion and the legal prohibition of all direct assaults upon it, becomes one of the most obvious and fundamental duties of the State.

The State and the Church, ed. John A. Ryan and M. F. X. Millar (New York: Macmillan, 1924)

729. Rev. Jimmy Swaggart

The Supreme Court of the United States of America is an institution damned by God Almighty.

Address, Washington, D.C., February 4, 1986

730. ———

It must never be forgotten that this is a Christian country based on the words of Almighty God.

Ibid.

APPENDIX 5
A SHARED
VISION

731. Religious Liberty in the 21st Century

Adopted on July 14, 1994

We join in issuing this statement at a time when America has reaffirmed its commitment to religious freedom through the Religious Freedom Restoration Act and is again recognizing the vital moral and spiritual role religion plays in both our public and private lives.

Yet, at the same time, we are confronted by two strikingly different views about the proper role of religion in public life. One portrays America as a Christian or Judeo-Christian nation. This view wrongly suggests that the Founders never meant to separate the institutions of church and state or to prohibit the establishment of religion. Such a view is historically inaccurate and endangers our common welfare because it uses religion to divide rather than unite the American people. This view of religion in public life, inaccurate and dangerous as it is, has gained credence in reaction to another inaccurate and equally damaging view of the proper role of religion in public life. The other view sees religion and religious groups as having a minimal role in—perhaps even being barred from—the vital public discourses we carry on as a democracy. It sees faith-based involvement in the democratic process as violating the principle of church-state separation. It regards religious arguments as naïve and seeks to embarrass any who profess religious motivation for their public positions on political issues. This view denies our country the powerful moral guidance of our religious heritage and discourages many of our brightest and most committed citizens from actively participating in our public life.

As individuals and organizations committed to religious liberty as well as a robust role for religion in public life, we share a different vision about the future: a vision that avoids both the theocratic tendencies on one side and the hostility toward religion associated with the other. Now more than ever, the United States must maintain its commitment to freedom for persons of all faiths or none. We are beset by religious and ethnic conflict abroad. Exploding pluralism challenges us at home. At such a time, we must reaffirm our dedication to providing what Roger Williams called a "haven for the cause of conscience." We agree with Williams that conscience is best guarded by maintaining a healthy distance between the institutions of religion and government.

But it is not enough to reaffirm these truths. We must incorporate them into our private lives as well as into our public policies. This statement is a call to action. We must apply these principles in practical ways whether we are electing a school board member or the President, whether we are debating aid to parochial schools or prayer in public schools.

THE CONSTITUTION

> *Congress shall make no law respecting an establishment of religion, or prohibiting the free exercise thereof . . .*

The first sixteen words of the First Amendment form the backbone of the American experiment. Together they guarantee religious liberty for Americans of every faith as well as for those who affirm no faith at all. A profound belief in the free exercise of religion motivated the decision of the Founders to disestablish religion in the new nation. The connecting link between the two clauses is freedom of conscience.

While not divorcing religion from public life, the establishment clause separates the institutions of church and state. Grounded in the belief that (1) government should serve all citizens regardless of their religious belief or disbelief, and

(2) authentic faith must be free and voluntary, the separation of church and state has been good for religion. This "lively experiment" has allowed American religions to flourish with unparalleled strength and diversity. The religious and ethnic diversity of the United States makes the constitutional prohibition against laws respecting an establishment of religion more important than ever. No one wants government taking sides against their religion in favor of someone else's. That principle cuts both ways. In matters of faith, government must not take sides at all.

Critics of the establishment clause argue that the phrase "separation of church and state" does not appear in the Constitution and that society cannot survive without government support of religion. As to the former, they are correct. "Separation of church and state," like "separation of powers," "fair trial" or even "religious freedom," does not appear in the Constitution. Yet, Article VI's prohibition against religious tests for public office and the establishment clause's prohibition against laws even "respecting" an establishment of religion makes clear that government is to be neutral in matters of faith. As to the latter, government support has proven a hindrance, not a help, to religion. History is replete with wrecked governments and wrecked churches brought down by the unhealthy union of church and state.

Some suggest that government support for religion should be permitted as long as no religion is favored over another and no citizen is forced to participate. The weight of the evidence suggests the Framers considered and rejected this approach. Even benign, non-coercive endorsements of religion make outsiders of those who are nonadherents of the prevailing faith. A proper interpretation of the establishment clause ensures that one's standing in the political community is not affected by one's standing in the religious community.

In practical terms, the separation of church and state requires that government refrain from promoting or inhibiting religion. Neutrality—by which religion is accommodated but never advocated by the state—should be the touchstone for interpreting both religion clauses.

The free exercise clause was designed to safeguard the inalienable right of Americans to believe, worship, and practice any faith we may choose without government interference. Subsumed in this right is the freedom to change our religious beliefs as we may see fit and to live according to our individual and communal beliefs. All faiths must be free to order their own internal affairs without governmental intrusion. No faith can ever be prohibited, penalized, or declared heretical by the government. All must be equally secure, minority as well as majority.

Like most constitutional rights, the free exercise of religion is not absolute. It cannot extend to practices that harm other human beings or threaten public safety and welfare. Absent some compelling reason, however, government should not be able to restrict religious exercise.

The free exercise clause can be only as vital and vibrant as the spirit of liberty abroad in the land. If that spirit is squelched or submerged, for whatever reason, the rights and freedoms of all citizens are at risk. In the words of the 1988 Williamsburg Charter: "A right for one is a right for another—and a responsibility for all."

Unfortunately, the Supreme Court's enforcement of the free exercise clause has been uneven over the years. While the Court has frequently reaffirmed the value of full and robust religious expression, it has occasionally failed to protect these important principles when faced with claims by unpopular or politically weak groups. For some, the protections promised under the free exercise clause have been all too fleeting.

Tragically, the Supreme Court's decision in *Employment Division* v. *Smith* (1990) weakened the free exercise clause even further. Describing the traditional legal protections for religion as a "luxury," the Court rolled back a half century of legal precedent. After *Smith*, the government in most cases was no longer required to demonstrate a compelling reason for restricting religious exercise.

Smith has been applied in dozens of free exercise cases around the country. The regrettable—though not unexpected—result has been that the citizen has lost almost every one of these cases. Orthodox Jews and Hmongs have been subjected to mandatory autopsies, violating their deeply held religious beliefs. Evangelical churches have been zoned out of residential areas, severely impeding their ability to worship. Churches have been subjected to historical landmarking laws as local governments attempted to dictate the configuration of their buildings. The rights of prisoners to freely exercise their religion have been routinely denied. After *Smith*, our "First Liberty" was not only no longer first, it was barely a liberty.

We applaud the passage of the Religious Freedom Restoration Act, which restores the protections for religious liberty stripped away by *Smith*. Thankfully, our system of checks and balances allows Congress to enact laws providing more protection for the exercise of religion than was recognized by the Supreme Court in *Smith*. Still, we long for the day when the Court again recognizes the exercise of religion as a fundamental constitutional right entitled to the highest level of legal protection.

RELIGION AND POLITICS

As concerned citizens, religious people should and do seek public office. As a conscience in society, religious organizations should and do seek to influence public policy. Separation of church and state does not mean the separation of religion and politics or, for that matter, of God and government.

While religious groups serve an important role in holding government accountable for its actions, that role can be maintained only when religion maintains a healthy distance from government.

Any attempt at affecting public policy should be tempered by a tolerance for differing views and a recognition that a multiplicity of voices is crucial for the success of a democratic society. Neither church nor state may control, dominate, or subjugate the other. Article VI of the Constitution wisely provides that no religious test shall be required for public office. Portraying America as a "Christian nation" violates the American commitment to both democratic government and religious liberty. Where religion is concerned, no person should be made to feel an outcast in his or her own land.

Accordingly, we must:

- Defend the right of religious individuals and organizations to speak, debate, and advocate openly in the public square;
- Stand firm by the principle that government action with a primary purpose or effect that advances religion violates the separation of church and state.

Similarly, we should:

- Discourage efforts to make a candidate's religious affiliation or nonaffiliation a campaign issue;
- Discourage candidates from invoking divine authority for their policies and platforms or from characterizing their opponents as sinful or ungodly.

RELIGION AND PUBLIC EDUCATION

One of the most critical issues facing our country is how best to educate our children. While recognizing the usefulness of private education, we affirm the particular importance of the public school system in accomplishing that task. Public schools belong to all citizens regardless of their faith perspectives. Public schools have the difficult task of equipping children for citizenship and transmitting to them our civil values.

The primary goal of the public schools is the education of children in an increasingly diverse society, not to provide a captive audience for the transmission of sectarian values. As a result, schools must not allow the public trust to be manipulated for religious goals. Schools are not to sponsor any religious exercises or to allow religious ceremonies at school-directed events. Public schools must remain neutral toward religion. As agents of the state, they must not promote or endorse any religion, or even religion in general. Nevertheless, public schools should accommodate the religious rights of students when that can be done without disrupting the learning process or interfering with the rights of others.

Applying these general principles, schools may teach about religion so long as it is accomplished from an academic, objective perspective that eschews all forms of proselytizing. Teaching about religion should occur when the subject naturally arises in the curriculum. We oppose interjecting religious beliefs into the curriculum at inappropriate points, such as attempting to teach creationism in biology class under the guise of science. Schools may not sponsor or encourage prayer or other devotional activities in the public classroom. They should not takes sides in religious disputes or suggest one religious tradition is superior to others. They should not teach in a way that undermines the student's sense of citizenship because he or she does not conform to a prescribed religious norm.

Nevertheless, schools should accommodate the free exercise rights of students. Private devotion or religious exercise on the part of the students, including private prayer, Bible reading or other religious activities, is permitted so long as they do not interfere with other students' rights or with the educational process. Schools should not discourage students from discussing their faith with other students except for reasonable time, place, and manner restrictions. While some of us disagree on the advisability of doing so, schools are generally free, under Supreme Court precedent, to permit a voluntary student religious group to meet and to allow release time programs off campus for religious studies without academic credit.

In sum, public schools should not advance religion, but should accommodate the free exercise of religion. They may not confer a benefit on religion but may lift governmentally imposed burdens on the free exercise of religion. They may not promote a religious perspective but may protect the religious exercise of students.

AID TO RELIGIOUS INSTITUTIONS

We agree with Jefferson and Madison that it is wrong to tax citizens to support the teaching of religion. In the words of the Virginia Statute for Establishing Religious Freedom: "No man shall be compelled to frequent or support any religious worship, place, or ministry whatsoever. . . ." Therefore, we oppose direct or indirect government funding of parochial schools at primary and secondary levels and of pervasively sectarian colleges and universities.

On the other hand, government aid to certain social service programs sponsored by religious organizations, such as homes for children and the elderly and hospitals, enjoys a long history. Aid to religious institutions that provide manifestly secular services (e.g., hospitals) does not pose a threat to religious liberty, if services are provided on a nondiscriminatory basis. However, if an institution indoctrinates its clients with religion, or discriminates based on religion in its admission policies, it should be deemed ineligible for government aid.

Some services are at the margins between education and social services and may require safeguards to protect church-state separation. Other questions arise when funded social services (e.g., foster homes or homes for the elderly) are residential in nature. In such cases government must arrange for residents' religious needs to be met, where possible, through access to existing ministries in the community.

Several broad and uniting principles should be applied in determining when it is appropriate for religious social services providers to receive government aid. Reference should be made to the types of institutions and services involved; the constituency to whom the services are provided; and the adequacy of church-state safeguards. Further, government's partnership with religious institutions for purposes of facilitating the availability of social services should recognize the nonfunded programs in those institutions need not operate under the same standards as publicly funded programs. Religious institutions receiving governmental funds for secular programs should be permitted, consistent with constitutional principles, to maintain their religious identities.

CONCLUSION

Our heritage of religious liberty and church-state separation must be reaffirmed. The increasing religious pluralism in our country beckons us to turn this heritage into a legacy. The aspirations of the Founders—that religion should involve a voluntary response and that government should remain neutral toward religion—must be converted into practical reality. Daniel Carroll of Maryland said it well over two hundred years ago when he declared that "the rights of conscience are . . . of particular delicacy and will little bear the gentlest touch of governmental hand." Carroll's lofty view of conscience captures our understanding of our past and guides our vision of the future. We commit ourselves to making this ideal a reality as we approach the twenty-first century.

Partial List of Signers

American Jewish Committee

American Jewish Congress

Americans for Religious Liberty

Baptist Joint Committee

Dr. B. Bert Beach

The Rev. Charles Bergstrom

The Rev. Dr. Joan Brown Campbell

Dr. Harvey Cox

Edd Doerr

The Rev. Dr. James M. Dunn

The Rev. Dr. Ronald B. Flowers

Richard T. Foltin

Bishop Edwin R. Garrison

Dr. Edwin S. Gaustad

The Rev. Elenora Giddings Ivory

The Rev. Dr. Stan Hastey

The Rev. Dean M. Kelley

Norman Lear

The Rev. Dr. Bill J. Leonard

National Council of Churches of Christ in the U.S.A.

People for the American Way

Dr. Richard Pierard

Samuel Rabinove

Rabbi David Saperstein

Marc D. Stern

The Rev. Dr. John Swomley

The Rev. Oliver S. Thomas

The Rev. J. Brent Walker

The Rev. Dr. Phillip Wogaman

APPENDIX 6

P RELIGION IN THE UBLIC SCHOOLS

732. A Joint Statement of Current Law, April 1995

The Constitution permits much private religious activity in and about the public schools. Unfortunately, this aspect of constitutional law is not as well known as it should be. Some say that the Supreme Court has declared the public schools "religion free zones" or that the law is so murky that school officials cannot know what is legally permissible. The former claim is simply wrong. And as to the latter, while there are some difficult issues, much has been settled. It is also unfortunately true that public school officials, due to their busy schedules, may not be as fully aware of this body of law as they could be. As a result, in some school districts some of these rights are not being observed.

The organizations whose names appear below span the ideological, religious, and political spectrum. They nevertheless share a commitment both to the freedom of religious practice and to the separation of church and state such freedom requires. In that spirit, we offer this statement of consensus on current law as an aid to parents, educators, and students.

Many of the organizations listed below are actively involved in litigation about religion in the schools. On some of the issues discussed in this summary, some of the organizations have urged the courts to reach positions different than they did. Though there are signatories on both sides which have and will press for different constitutional treatments of some of the topics discussed below, they all agree that the following is an accurate statement of what the law currently is.

STUDENT PRAYERS

1. Students have the right to pray individually or in groups or to discuss their religious views with their peers so long as they are not disruptive. Because the Establishment Clause does not apply to purely private speech, students enjoy the right to read their Bibles or other scriptures, say grace before meals, pray before tests, and discuss religion with other willing student listeners. In the classroom students have the right to pray quietly except when required to be actively engaged in school activities (for example, students may not decide to pray just as a teacher calls on them). In informal settings, such as the cafeteria or in the halls, students may pray either audibly or silently, subject to the same rules of order as apply to other speech in these locations. However, the right to engage in voluntary prayer does not include, for example, the right to have a captive audience listen or to compel other students to participate.

GRADUATION PRAYER AND BACCALAUREATES

2. School officials may not mandate or organize prayer at graduation, nor may they organize a religious baccalaureate ceremony. If the school generally rents out its facilities to private groups, it must rent them out on the same terms, and on a first-come, first-served basis, to organizers of privately sponsored religious baccalaureate services, provided that the school does not extend preferential treatment to the baccalaureate ceremony and the school disclaims official endorsement of the program.

3. The courts have reached conflicting conclusions under the federal Constitution on student-initiated prayer at graduation. Until the issue is authoritatively resolved, schools should ask their lawyers what rules apply in their area.

OFFICIAL PARTICIPATION OR ENCOURAGEMENT OF RELIGIOUS ACTIVITY

4. Teachers and school administrators, when acting in those capacities, are representatives of the state, and, in those capacities, are themselves prohibited from encouraging or soliciting student religious or anti-religious activity. Similarly, when acting in their official capacities, teachers may not engage in religious activities with their students. However, teachers may engage in private religious activity in faculty lounges.

TEACHING ABOUT RELIGION

5. Students may be taught about religion, but public schools may not teach religion. As the U.S. Supreme Court has repeatedly said, "It might well be said that one's education is not complete without a study of comparative religion, or the history of religion and its relationship to the advancement of civilization." It would be difficult to teach art, music, literature, and most social studies without considering religious influences.

The history of religion, comparative religion, the Bible (or other scripture) as literature (either as a separate course or within some other existing course) are all permissible public school subjects. It is both permissible and desirable to teach objectively about the role of religion in the history of the United States and other countries. One can teach that the pilgrims came to this country with a particular religious vision, that Catholics and others have been subjected to persecution or that many of those participating in the abolitionist, women's suffrage, and civil rights movements had religious motivations.

6. These same rules apply to the recurring controversy surrounding theories of evolution. Schools may teach about explanations of life on earth, including religious ones (such as "creationism"), in comparative religion or social studies classes. In science class, however, they may present only genuinely scientific critiques of, or evidence for, any explanation of life on earth, but not religious critiques (beliefs unverifiable by scientific methodology). Schools may not refuse to teach evolutionary theory in order to avoid giving offense to reli-

gion nor may they circumvent these rules by labeling as science an article of religious faith. Public schools must not teach as scientific fact or theory any religious doctrine, including "creationism," although any genuinely scientific evidence for or against any explanation of life may be taught. Just as they may neither advance nor inhibit any religious doctrine, teachers should not ridicule, for
example, a student's religious explanation for life on earth.

STUDENT ASSIGNMENTS AND RELIGION

7. Students may express their religious beliefs in the form of reports,
homework, and artwork, and such expressions are constitutionally protected.
Teachers may not reject or correct such submissions simply because they include
a religious symbol or address religious themes. Likewise, teachers may not
require students to modify, include, or excise religious views in their assignments, if germane. These assignments should be judged by ordinary academic
standards of substance, relevance, appearance, and grammar.

8. Somewhat more problematic from a legal point of view are other public
expressions of religious views in the classroom. Unfortunately for school officials, there are traps on either side of this issue, and it is possible that litigation
will result no matter what course is taken. It is easier to describe the settled cases
than to state clear rules of law. Schools must carefully steer between the claims
of student speakers who assert a right to express themselves on religious subjects
and the asserted rights of student listeners to be free of unwelcome religious persuasion in a public school classroom.

    a.   Religious or anti-religious remarks made in the ordinary course of
classroom discussion or student presentations are permissible and constitute a protected right. If in a sex education class a student remarks
that abortion should be illegal because God has prohibited it, a teacher
should not silence the remark, ridicule it, rule it out of bounds, or
endorse it, any more than a teacher may silence a student's religious
based comment in favor of choice.

    b.   If a class assignment calls for an oral presentation on a subject of the
student's choosing, and, for example, the student responds by conducting a religious service, the school has the right—as well as the

duty—to prevent itself from being used as a church. Other students are not voluntarily in attendance and cannot be forced to become an unwilling congregation.

c.   Teachers may rule out-of-order religious remarks that are irrelevant to the subject at hand. In a discussion of Hamlet's sanity, for example, a student may not interject views on creationism.

DISTRIBUTION OF RELIGIOUS LITERATURE

9.   Students have the right to distribute religious literature to their school-mates, subject to those reasonable time, place, and manner or other constitutionally acceptable restrictions imposed on the distribution of all non-school literature. Thus, a school may confine distribution of all literature to a particular table at particular times. It may not single out religious literature for burdensome regulation.

10.   Outsiders may not be given access to the classroom to distribute religious or anti-religious literature. No court has yet considered whether, if all other community groups are permitted to distribute literature in common areas of public schools, religious groups must be allowed to do so on equal terms subject to reasonable time, place, and manner restrictions.

'SEE YOU AT THE POLE'

11.   Student participation in before- or after-school events, such as "see you at the pole," is permissible. School officials, acting in an official capacity, may neither discourage nor encourage participation in such an event.

RELIGIOUS PERSUASION VERSUS RELIGIOUS HARASSMENT

12.   Students have the right to speak to, and attempt to persuade, their peers about religious topics just as they do with regard to political topics. But

school officials should intercede to stop student religious speech if it turns into religious harassment aimed at a student or a small group of students. While it is constitutionally permissible for a student to approach another and issue an invitation to attend church, repeated invitations in the face of a request to stop constitute harassment. Where this line is to be drawn in particular cases will depend on the age of the students and other circumstances.

EQUAL ACCESS ACT

13. Student religious clubs in secondary schools must be permitted to meet and to have equal access to campus media to announce their meetings, if a school receives federal funds and permits any student non-curricular club to meet during non-instructional time. This is the command of the Equal Access Act. A non-curricular club is any club not related directly to a subject taught or soon-to-be taught in the school. Although schools have the right to ban all non-curriculum clubs, they may not dodge the law's requirement by the expedient of declaring all clubs curriculum-related. On the other hand, teachers may not actively participate in club activities and "non-school persons" may not control or regularly attend club meetings.

The Act's constitutionality has been upheld by the Supreme Court, rejecting claims that the Act violates the Establishment Clause. The Act's requirements are described in more detail in *The Equal Access Act and the Public Schools: Questions and Answers on the Equal Access Act,* a pamphlet published by a broad spectrum of religious and civil liberties groups.

RELIGIOUS HOLIDAYS

14. Generally, public schools may teach about religious holidays and may celebrate the secular aspects of the holiday and objectively teach about their religious aspects. They may not observe the holidays as religious events. Schools should generally excuse students who do not wish to participate in holiday events. Those interested in further details should see *Religious Holidays in the Public Schools: Questions and Answers,* a pamphlet published by a broad spectrum of religious and civil liberties groups.

EXCUSAL FROM RELIGIOUSLY OBJECTIONABLE LESSONS

15. Schools enjoy substantial discretion to excuse individual students from lessons which are objectionable to that students or to his or her parent on the basis of religion. Schools can exercise that authority in ways which would defuse many conflicts over curriculum content. If it is proved that particular lessons substantially burden a student's free exercise of religion and if the school cannot prove a compelling interest in requiring attendance the school would be legally required to excuse the student.

TEACHING VALUES

16. Schools may teach civic virtues, including honesty, good citizenship, sportsmanship, courage, respect for the rights and freedoms of others, respect for persons and their property, civility, the dual virtues of morality and tolerance, and hard work. Subject to whatever rights of excusal exist (see number fifteen above) under the federal Constitution and state law, schools may teach sexual abstinence and contraception; whether and how schools teach these sensitive subjects is a matter of educational policy. However, these may not be taught as religious tenets. The mere fact that most, if not all, religions also teach these values does not make it unlawful to teach them.

STUDENT GARB

17. Religious messages on T-shirts and the like may not be singled out for suppression. Students may wear religious attire, such as yarmulkes and head scarves, and they may not be forced to wear gym clothes that they regard, on religious grounds, as immodest.

RELEASED TIME

18. Schools have the discretion to dismiss students to off-premises religious instruction, provided that schools do not encourage or discourage participation or penalize those who do not attend. Schools may not allow religious instruction by outsiders on premises during the school day.

Drafting Committee

American Jewish Congress, chair
American Civil Liberties Union
American Jewish Committee
American Muslim Council
Anti-Defamation League
Baptist Joint Committee
Christian Legal Society

General Conference of Seventh-day Adventists
National Association of Evangelicals
National Council of Churches
People for the American Way
Union of American Hebrew Congregations

ENDORSING ORGANIZATIONS

American Ethical Union
American Humanist Association
Americans for Religious Liberty
Americans United for Separation of Church and State
B'nai B'rith International
Christian Science Church
Church of the Brethren, Washington Office
Church of Scientology International
Evangelical Lutheran Church in America, Lutheran Office of Governmental Affairs
Federation of Reconstructionist Congregations and Havurot
Friends Committee on National Legislation
Guru Gobind Singh Foundation
Interfaith Alliance

Interfaith Impact for Justice and Peace
National Council of Jewish Women
National Jewish Community Relations Advisory Council (NJCRAC)
National Ministries, American Baptist Churches, USA
National Sikh Center
North American Council for Muslim Women
Presbyterian Church, USA
Reorganized Church of Jesus Christ of Latter Day Saints
Unitarian Universalist Association of Congregations
United Church of Christ, Office for Church in Society

INDEX

www.ingramcontent.com/pod-product-compliance
Lightning Source LLC
Chambersburg PA
CBHW072102020426
42334CB00017B/1600